The Aerofilms Book of
IRELAND
— FROM THE AIR —

The Aerofilms Book of
IRELAND
— FROM THE AIR —
Benedict Kiely

Weidenfeld and Nicolson
London

Photo enlargements

All the pictures in this book are available as photographic enlargements from the original negative. They were selected from several thousand photographs taken at the same time, all of which are also available, as are a selection of black and white prints taken in the 1950s and 1960s and many pre-1939 pictures.

Free proofs and price list from:
Aerofilms Limited, Gate Studios, Station Road, Borecham Wood, Herts WD6 1EJ

Photographs copyright © 1985 Aerofilms Ltd
Text copyright © 1985 Benedict Kiely

First paperback edition published 1990

First published in Great Britain by
George Weidenfeld and Nicolson Ltd
91 Clapham High Street
London SW4 7TA

Map on page 6 by Line and Line

Transparencies made by
Copeland, Douglas & Dyer from
original colour negatives
Typeset by Keyspools Ltd, Golborne, Lancashire
Colour separations by Newsele Litho Ltd
Printed in Italy by LEGO, Vicenza

ISBN 0 297 83084 8

Contents

Map 6

Introduction 7

Tory Island

Dunfanaghy
Sheephaven
Grianan of Aileach

Lough Swilly
Malin
Buncrana
Rathmullan

Portrush
Mussenden House
Lough Foyle
Coleraine

Dunluce Castle

ANTRIM

Derry

DONEGAL

LONDONDERRY

River Bann

MOUNTAINS
OF ANTRIM

Strabane
Sion Mills

TYRONE

Omagh

Belfast

Barnesmore Gap
Donegal
Station Island

Lough Derg

ULSTER

River Lagan

Lough Neagh

Donegal Bay
Mullaghmore
Inishmurray

Belleek

Lower Lough Erne

DOWN

Lissadell
Benbulben
Rosses Point
Sligo Bay
Sligo

FERMANAGH
Monaghan

Armagh
ARMAGH

River Newry

Newry
Slieve Donard

Upper Lough Erne
Crossmaglen

Mourne Mountains
Carlingford Lough

Bellacorick

SLIGO
Keschcorran

Lough Allen

MONAGHAN
Lough Muckno

Lough Key LEITRIM
Boyle
Drumsna

Cavan
Bellamont Forest
Dundalk

Achill Island
Achill Sound

MAYO

Lough Ramor

CAVAN

Ballyjamesduff
Lough Gowna

LOUTH
Monasterboice

Clare Island
Clew Bay
Westport
Croagh Patrick

ROSCOMMON

LONGFORD

Hill of Lloyd
Lough Derryvaragh

Drogheda
River Boyne
Newgrange
Clogherhead

CONNACHT

Lough Mask

Abbeyshrule
Clonyn Castle
Trim

Hill of Tara

Ashford Castle

GALWAY

River Inny
WESTMEATH
Athlone

MEATH

Lambay Island

Lough Corrib

Maynooth
Castletown House
Allenwood
Straffan Lodge

Dublin
River Liffey

Bulloch Harbour
Sandycove
Dun Laoghaire
Killiney

Galway

Kilconnel Friary
Shannonbridge

Clonmacnoise
OFFALY

DUBLIN

Aran Islands
Galway Bay
Tawin Island

River Shannon

The Curragh
KILDARE

Powerscourt
Sugarloaf Mountain
Leamore Strand

Inishmore
Inishmaan
Inisheer
Cliffs of Moher

The Burren
Caherconnell
Lisdoonvarna

Thoor Ballylee

Birr
Birr Castle
Rock of Dunamase

Emo Park

Blessington
Reservoir

Wicklow

LAOIS LEINSTER

WICKLOW

CLARE

Monahincha

WICKLOW
MOUNTAINS

Bunratty Castle

Castlecomer
Kilkenny

CARLOW

Aughinish
Limerick

TIPPERARY

KILKENNY

WEXFORD

LIMERICK

Athassel Abbey
Cashel

Jerpoint Abbey
St Mullin's

Enniscorthy

Tipperary

River Nore
River Barrow
New Ross

KERRY

Ballyporeen

MUNSTER

River Suir
WATERFORD

Wexford

Knockmealdown Mountains
River Blackwater

Waterford
Tramore

Kilmore Quay

Great Blasket

Dingle Bay Inisfallen Abbey Killarney
Lough Leane Ross Castle
Macgillycuddy's Reeks

CORK

Lismore Castle

Blarney Castle

Cobh

Cork
Spike Island

Kinsale

Whiddy Island

Bantry Bay

Skibbereen

Introduction

Was it Dean Stanley, a most reverend Englishman, who said, as he approached the end, that things seemed different when you assumed the horizontal? And we all do know that if you stand on your head on the top of a high hill, the colours of the landscape stand out more vividly. But many years spent travelling the roads of Ireland, first out of curiosity, later of necessity and as a journalist, did in no way prepare me for the View from Above. Things seem different when you assume the stance, or the seat, of the Deity, and it could be that many of the problems of our world result from that undeniable truth.

Consider, for instance, the Rock of Cashel, which halts you in your stride as you go south from Dublin. You must look up to Cashel as you would look up to heaven to see, in the monastic past, the prince of Cashel, prelate and king, blessing the bread and chalice, earth's holiest offering. For man to attempt, in this case, to share the view of the angels might well be regarded as presumption.

But our vision of the Hill of Tara in royal Meath is another matter. Tara, when you first walk on it, is a sadness and a disillusion, for the halls of this historic seat of the ancient Kings of Ireland have crumbled away. Seen from above, however, a pattern begins to emerge, and it becomes almost possible to believe that that green place was once, truly, the abode of kings.

Towns and cities on good rivers have, of course, a considerable advantage when posing for aerial pictures. Cork and Limerick are specially blessed, and Belfast has the Lagan and the Lough. And it is interesting to note how, say, in the case of Omagh the river dictated the growth and shape of the town and the line and length of its long main street, two streets joined.

By the flying camera even the most secretive landscape can be forced into a sort of frankness. That vision of the Corrib Canal that never was a canal might come out of some wonder-tale. As in a way it does. And the extent and the flatness of the peatbogs can here be fully appreciated. To Jane Barlow, writing her stories at the beginning of the century, they were places of melancholy beauty. Stripped naked by the machine and viewed from on high, they belong with the vast Serbonian bog, where armies whole have sunk.

Everything in Ireland, I once said, reminds me of something else, which may be because of the compelling fragmentation of our landscape and history or, merely, because of the wandering state of my own mind. There was once a sentimental, religious and patriotic song, halfway to hymnology, about an Irish exile dying somewhere and enquiring with his last gasp, 'Will my soul pass through old Ireland on the way to meet its God?', and whether the soul would see this place or that. With the aid not of archangels but of Aerofilms, and going over this place and that, I am impressed by the multitude and complexity of emotions and memories these images stir in me, some out of history, some out of my own experience. This is a small island and I seem to have been around for a long time.

The poet Patrick Kavanagh, whom I have mentioned here more than once, wrote of 'the undying difference in the corner of a field'. If here you do not find that particular corner of field or town, or river-bend or roadway, in which you have meditated on that undying difference, then kindly put the lack down to limitations of space – for everything human has its limitations.

My thanks to my friend Sean J. White, Dean of the School of Irish Studies, for his help and scholarly advice, and with the customary proviso that any errors are my responsibility.

Benedict Kiely
Donnybrook, Dublin, 1985

Ulster

Portrush, Antrim ▷

When I was growing up, say 1919–37, in the North, the Protestants went to see the sea at Portrush in County Antrim, the Catholics at Bundoran in County Donegal. The sea was sectarian. That may no longer be the case – not to that extent. The deep and dark blue ocean has liberalized. Some day the land may follow.

Portrush is a fine town and has famous golf clubs in the vicinity; and if you want to visit the Giant's Causeway or Dunluce Castle, or to drink Bushmills, or to go fishing on the broad River Bann, there's no better place to begin. Except, perhaps, Portstewart.

Dunluce Castle, Antrim ▷

When genteel travellers set out, as in Lady Morgan's novel *O'Donnell* (1814), to play the pilgrim to 'that great shrine of Nature', the Giant's Causeway on the Antrim coast, they inevitably took in the Gothic wonder of Dunluce Castle, and perhaps also the village of Bushmills where the whiskey comes from. Too much Bushmills might make Dunluce too perilous.

Only a quite neurotic insistence on security could have impelled anyone to build a castle in such a place. Yet there seems to have been a fort there from the earliest times. Dun Lios, the somewhat tautological name, may be quite fairly interpreted as The Strong Fort. Admission by invitation only.

The remains that we see here now, or part of them, may date back for seven hundred years, to the Norman Richard de Burgo, Earl of Ulster, or some of his entourage. Over the centuries, as is the way in such cases, this desirable seaside residence changed hands: the MacQuillans acquired it, and later the De Mandevilles, who were overthrown *c.*1560 by the renowned Scots freebooters the MacDonnells from across the water, later Earls of Antrim. Survivors of wrecked ships of the Spanish Armada were offered sanctuary at Dunluce by Sorley Boy MacDonnell, Lord of Dunluce. The MacDonnells abandoned the castle after the 1641 rebellion. Their lineal descendants handed it over to the Northern Ireland Government as a National Monument in 1928.

On one celebrated occasion part of the servants' quarters fell into the sea, along with a quantity of servants. But domestic help was in abundance at the time.

◁ Belfast City, Antrim

'This is my country. If my people came from England here four centuries ago, the only trace that's left is in my name. Kilmore, Armagh, no other sod can show the weathered stone of our first burying. Born in Belfast which drew the landless in, that river-straddling, hill-rimmed town, I cling to the inflexions of my origin.'

That was the poet, John Hewitt, about whom one can say, without flattery, that in him all that is best in the North and in Belfast unite in one man and in his poetry.

That river-straddling, hill-rimmed town centres here around Donegal Square and the huge City Hall, which looks as if it had been there forever, but which, designed by Sir Brumwell Thomas, went up as recently as 1906. Its air of antiquity may be due simply to its overwhelming size and its Renaissance style. Queen Victoria, on a comparable scale, sits beside it and there is the Royal Irish Rifles memorial statue of the first Marquess of Dufferin and Ava. Almost opposite it is the Linenhall Library (Belfast grew up on linen), dating from the late eighteenth century. The first librarian was Thomas Russell, the United Irishman, friend and fellow rebel of Robert Emmet, who was executed in Dublin for high treason in 1803.

Not far from the City Hall is the Grand Opera House, designed by the theatre architect, Frank Matcham, its fine Rococo interior now fully and splendidly restored. And in Great Victoria Street is one of the gems of the city, the Crown Bar, a nineteenth-century pub preserved by the National Trust.

Edward Carson, a lawyer and a Dubliner of Italian origin, led the signing in the City Hall in 1909 of the Covenant against Home Rule for Ireland. Cane Hill looked down on it all, and on MacArt's fort, a medieval earthwork where, at the end of the eighteenth century, Theobald Wolfe Tone and friends dreamed of an Irish republic, French style. The City Hall is still there and MacArt's fort. Carson still stands at the foot of the slope before Stormont Castle.

A Dubliner may be bourgeois enough to talk about going into Town. A Belfastman will say The City. No matter what his other beliefs may be, he has it as an article of faith that there is one city in the world.

Belfast, God and the rest of us know, has its problems. Belfast has its proper pride. Belfast is The City. Search for it in the works of Michael McFaverty, Joseph Tomelty, Bernard McLaverty, Michael Longley, Derek Mahon and others.

▽ Harland and Wolf Shipyards, Belfast, Antrim

The River Lagan opens out to Belfast Lough and the Lough opens out to the Irish Sea, and there, where the Lagan melts into the Lough, and on the Queen's Island, are the shipyards of Harland and Wolff, where some of the world's most splendid ships have had their origins.

The names alone of all the ships in whose building Andrews had a hand, more or less, as designer, constructor, supervisor and adviser, would fill this page. The *Cedric*, the *Baltic*, the *Adriatic*, the *Oceanic*, the *Amerika*, the *President Lincoln*, the *President Grant*, the *Nieuw Amsterdam*, the *Rotterdam*, the *Lapland* – those are a few of them. Their names are as familiar to us as those of our friends. We have, some of us, seen the great ships on whose bows they are inscribed, perhaps sailed in them, or watched anxiously for their arrival at some port of the world . . .

That positively lyrical passage was written as long ago as 1912, by Shaun F. Bullock, the Fermanagh novelist, telling the story of Thomas Andrews, shipbuilder, who sent out so many ships and who went with one of them, the *Titanic*, to what Wordsworth would have called the incommunicable sleep – and went, as witnesses told, heroically.

Airliners have all but replaced the ocean-going liners and the shipyards have adapted. But the story of Thomas Andrews still remains an inspiration.

Armagh City, Armagh ▷

Fifty-five years ago, when I first visited the primatial city of Armagh, my heart was torn with envy of my ten-year-old Armagh contemporaries who had the freedom of the beautiful oval greenery of the Mall. It seemed then like the eighth wonder. At that age I was less impressed, not knowing a thing about it, by the long and complicated ecclesiastical history of the place and by the way in which that history was represented by the two cathedrals, outfacing each other from their own private hilltops: the soaring Catholic nineteenth-century cathedral, a symbol of renaissance in the centre of the picture; the Protestant cathedral, after many vicissitudes on the site where Patrick placed his foundation.

The city itself is a treasure-house for those who value Georgian-Regency architecture, and on the dim horizon history fades out into pre-Christian times. Eamhain Macha (Navan Fort) about two miles to the west, was the seat of the ancient kings of Ulster. Armagh is Ard Macha or Macha's High Place and Macha was a goddess who was there before Patrick, or cardinal or archbishop. And Eamhain Macha was the hub of the great saga tales of the Ulster heroes, Cuchulain and company.

Crossmaglen, Armagh ▷

There is a possibility, I have heard it said, that if the Duke of Wellington had been in charge when the present troubles began, he would have rebuilt the earthworks of Torres Vedras, withdrawn his troops, and let anyone who willed, or could, rule Crossmaglen. For here in South Armagh, and close to Slieve Gullion mountain, is tough, rugged, independent country, still with a strong Gaelic tradition even if the language has died there.

And the horse-dealers of Crossmaglen, a famous breed, are renowned in the poem about the innocent country boy who went to the horsefair and found that his tea had been tampered with:

> I was a bold teetotaller for nine long years or
>   more,
> The neighbours all respected me, and decent
>   clothes I wore.
> My parents they were fond of me, 'till one
>   unlucky day,
> Just like a child, I was beguiled by whiskey in me
>   tay.
> It wasn't the lads from Shercock, nor the boys
>   from Ballybay,
> But the dalin' men from Crossmaglen put
>   whiskey in me tay.

A few miles away and south of the Border, in County Monaghan, is Inniskeen, the home-village of the poet Patrick Kavanagh.

◁ **Loch Gowna**, Cavan

So much of the counties of Cavan and Fermanagh is a filigree pattern of green fields and glistening water. Here it begins in Loch Gowna in Cavan and drifts on, slightly west of north, by Upper Lough Erne and the town of Belturbet to Enniskillen and then the majestic reaches of the Lower Erne. On the island of Inchmore in Lough Gowna there is a Columban monastic site, later an Augustinian monastery, and a bronze bell from that monastery is preserved in the Catholic church at Aughnacliff on the mainland. For angling holidays the nearest towns are Arvagh, County Cavan, and Granard, County Longford; but there is also the pretty little village of Gowna, home of the great ballad-singer Margaret O'Reilly.

Lough Ramor, Cavan ▷

This lovely lake is the source of the Leinster River Blackwater which joins the Boyne by Navan: and about both rivers, as elsewhere mentioned, Sir William Wilde, father of Oscar, wrote his classical *Beauties of the Boyne and Blackwater*. The lake adds status to the town of Virginia, which is on the main road from Cavan town to Dublin, and which came into existence during the Ulster Plantation; it was named, almost inevitably, after the Virgin Queen.

Not far away is the site of Cuilcagh House, where the Rev. Thomas Sheridan (1687–1783) lived. He was the friend of Swift, father of the actor and author Thomas Sheridan, and grandfather of Richard Brinsley Sheridan. In Cuilcagh House Swift wrote *Gulliver's Travels*.

Bellamont Forest, Cootehill, Cavan

If you turn to the left at the Bridge of Finnea and stop when halfway to Cootehill, you will find the Garden of Eden in Ballyjamesduff. And if you grow weary of Eden or are expelled, as better people were before you, go the rest of the way to the handsome and hospitable town of Cootehill, one of my favourite small towns, and to Bellamont Forest, the stately eighteenth-century building which was formerly the residence of Brigadier Dorman O Gowan. Before that it housed the Coote family, who gave their name to the town.

Bellamont Forest is one of the finest of all Palladian houses in these islands. It was built *c.* 1730 for Thomas Coote, Lord Justice of the King's Bench in Ireland, to the designs of his nephew, Sir Edward Lovett Pearce, and was inspired by Palladio's villas at Vicenza and Montagna. Charles Coote, Thomas's grandson – a rather ridiculous figure and a famous womanizer – inherited the house in 1766, and a year later became Earl of Bellamont, whereupon he changed the name of the house from Coote Hill to Bellamont Forest.

Close to the town of Cootehill is Annaghmaker-rig, once the home of Sir Tyrone Guthrie, now a house of study for writers and artists.

Ballyjamesduff, Cavan

Percy French, gentleman, poet and singer, was most certainly here in this Cavan countryside of the little lakes, and quite close to the two large and lovely stretches of water – Loughs Ramor and Sheelin:

> The Garden of Eden has vanished, they say,
> But I know the lie of it still.
> Just turn to the left at the Bridge of Finnea
> And stop when halfway to Cootehill.
> 'Tis there you will find it, I'll go, sure enough,
> When fortune has come to my call,

> For the grass it grows around Ballyjamesduff,
> And the blue sky is over it all.
> And tones that are tender, and tones that are
>   rough
> Are whispering over the sea:
> 'Come back, Paddy Reilly, to Ballyjamesduff,
> Come home, Paddy Reilly, to me.'

Local people say, simply, Ballyduff, half-eliminating the Black James who gave the place its name. He was a Sir James Duff who commanded British troops during the 1798 Rebellion.

Cavan Town, Cavan

'The Brenny plains are wide, and there are banners where I ride', wrote the poet Pádraic Colum who, although he lived most of his life in New York, had left his heart most decidedly in the ancient land of Breifne. Nearly seven hundred years ago the Lord of East Brenny (Breifne) founded here a Franciscan friary. This is the heart of O'Reilly country and the friary is no longer to be found, having been thoroughly, and several times, burnt out by the English in the fifteenth and sixteenth centuries. But in the hallowed precincts many men of the Clan O'Reilly were, after life's turbulence, laid to rest, including the legendary Myles the Slasher O'Reilly who, in 1646, fell in battle at the Bridge of Finea where the River Inny emerges from Lough Sheelin.

There also was laid the body of Owen Roe O'Neill, officer from the European wars who, in one of the dreams of the Irish mind, might have been able to disrupt the peripateticism of Cromwell had not he been poisoned, as is widely believed. Well, poison was in good supply at the time:

> Did they dare, did they dare to slay Owen Roe
>   O'Neill,
> Yea, they slew him with poison whom they
>   feared to meet with steel.

Legendary people lived here: that is if legendary people ever lived anywhere. The Fomorians, a sort of cyclopean people who move in the mists of our pre-history, 'a race of pirates who infested the coasts of Ireland and oppressed the inhabitants', were said to have had their principal stronghold on Tory Island in the ultimate north-west. Their reputed leader was Balor of the Blows and of the Evil Eye, only one eye, and bang in the middle of his forehead. So I have been told. Two of the tower-like rocks to the east of the island are called Balor's Fort and Balor's Prison.

Colmcille, great saint of Donegal and Derry and Iona, passed that way in the sixth century, and there are fragments of a round tower and a high cross, and some other details.

There are also, or were, the cursing stones. There is a fable, not too popular among the islanders, that in 1884 the stones were used when the British gunboat *Wasp* set out for Tory to help collect the rates. The *Wasp* sank with loss of life.

Flann O'Brien used to say: 'They prayed. Only God and themselves know who they prayed to. But the *Wasp* sank.'

Tory today, like many a small island, struggles for survival.

Donegal Town, Donegal ▷

The town of Donegal, Fort of the Foreigners, gives its name to the county, or rather the original fort did. The foreigners were, most likely, Vikings. There is a story, recorded in the tenth century, in a poem by a Donegal bard, of how Egnahan, father of Donnell (who was, perhaps, father of all the O'Donnells), gave his three daughters, Duvlin, Bebua and Bebuin in a peace-making marriage to three Vikings. We may only hope that they kept the peace.

But the Vikings are pale, remote ghosts when compared with the great Clan O Domhnaill. A long succession of chieftains of that name made this place, at the mouth of the river Eske, their home and fortress, built their castle, founded in 1474 the Franciscan friary, and defended the place against the English until the final defeat of O'Neill and O'Donnell at the Battle of Kinsale.

The friars in the course of the years and the wars moved from place to place, and at Bundrowes, further down the coast, where the Drowes River comes from Lough Melvin to the sea, four Franciscans commenced the great work *The Annals of the Four Masters* that gives lustre to this part of Ireland. Their work was done between 1630 and 1636. They were Michael O Clery, Peregrine O Clery, Peregrine Duignan and Fearfeasa O Mulconry, names forever to be honoured.

◁ **Buncrana,** Donegal

Of all the many inlets of the sea that break into the much-indented shore of this island, Lough Swilly is among the most impressive. To the east, between the Swilly and Loch Foyle, is the peninsula of Inishowen, a land to itself, where the O'Dohertys tall from dark Donegal were lords. Here, near the town and seaside resort of Buncrana, they had, in ancient times, a castle. Those industrious incendiaries, the English, burned it in 1608 when Sir Cahir O'Doherty rebelled against the Crown, but then everybody was burning up everybody in those days. Car bombs had not been invented.

Somewhere nearby on the Loch, and between Buncrana and Rathmullan on the far shore, Theobald Wolfe Tone was taken off a French ship in 1798, to die in prison in Dublin either by murder or by his own hand. He touched land hereabouts as a prisoner.

There's a fine song about Glenswilly. Two of the lines could have a message for our times:

> May peace and plenty reign supreme
>   along Lough Swilly shore.
> May discord never enter our Irish homes no
>   more.

Dunfanaghy, Donegal ▷

Sixty years ago the eminent George Russell (known as AE), poet, philosopher, painter, friend of Arthur Balfour, and organizer of cooperative creameries, wrote from the neighbourhood of Dunfanaghy to a friend and said that Ireland was a very small and unimportant part of the planet, and that he did not share the egomania of his fellow countrymen who thought that the whole world was staring at them. 'But,' he went on, 'it is a lovely country to live in, and here in a little cottage on a hill-farm I can see seven seas as I look around through the gaps in the hills and rocks . . .'

So there are the seven seas and the many-armed bays, and the fine town of Dunfanaghy, and tucked in here and there along the coast are Falcarragh and Portnablagh and Creeslough. And protecting them all from the ocean are Horn Head and MacSwine's Gun, a marine tunnel through which the sea used to boom with a thunderous roar, a sound that could be heard for miles. But the last I heard of the Gun was that the rock structure had weakened, and with it the boom.

◁ **Station Island,** Lough Derg, Donegal

This is the pilgrims' lake and the pilgrims' island, and the scene of St Patrick's purgatory, and W.B.Yeats wrote of the 'grey island consecrated by the verse of Calderon and the feet of twelve centuries of pilgrims'. Men and women who believe in prayer and in penance still go there in thousands every year: a sanative sight in the world we survive in. And many Irish writers have, from various points of view, considered this island on which tradition says that Patrick prayed: William Carleton, W.B.Yeats, Shane Leslie, Sean O'Faolain, Denis Devlin. Most recently, Seamus Heaney has inclined his head in that direction in his splendid 'Station Island'.

This is the Donegal Lough Derg, not to be confused, if such a confusion were possible, with the vast lake on the Shannon between Portumna and Killaloe.

Rathmullan, Donegal ▷

In the September of 1607, the few people around here at the time were in mourning for the passing of Gaelic Ireland. They did not at that moment see it in that way. How could they? What they did see was that the Great O'Neill, Hugh of Tyrone, and Rúairí O'Donnell, successor of Red Hugh of Tyrconnell, and their entourage had sailed from Rathmullan for Europe after the failure of the Irish rebellion of 1595, preferring a life of exile to one of undignified submission to the English.

Today Rathmullan is as we see it: a small, bright town and a holiday place.

Malin, Donegal ▷

The late Patrick Boyle, novelist and writer of stories, used to say that one of the interesting things about Magilligan Strand, in County Derry, was that you could stand there in Northern Ireland and look due north at the South of Ireland.

What Pat Boyle was talking about was Malin Head, the most northerly point of the island of Ireland; and tucked in behind it, on the Culdaff River, perhaps the greatest small river in Ireland for the running of the white trout, is the village of Malin.

It is one of the few villages in Ireland that has, as in England or in portions of France, a perfectly triangular village green, geese and all. A lovely place to dream in.

△ **Doe Castle,** Sheephaven Bay

On a rocky point on Sheephaven Bay, one of the three great inlets of north Donegal (the other two being Mulroy and Swilly) MacSuibhne na dtuath kept his fortress: Doe Castle, as it is now commonly called. The great chieftain is also familiarly remembered as MacSwiney of the Battleaxes.

The MacSwineys might be regarded, perhaps, as a tributary sept of the O'Donnells, if that proud and warlike family would have acknowledged supremacy to anyone: and the young Prince Red Hugh O'Donnell was, according to ancient Gaelic custom, reared here in fosterage. In the course of that fosterage Red Hugh was, we are told tricked on board an English vessel and swept away to captivity in Dublin Castle. He escaped to tell the tale and passed through Omagh on the way home, crossing the Owenreagh (Drumragh) river at Lissan bridge. Neither Omagh nor Lissan bridge were there at the time.

Donegal people are a very tidy, half-Scottish people, as may be seen in the pattern of the fields beyond Doe, a carefulness that is always a pleasure to contemplate.

The glimmering blue spot in the distance is Glen Lough, a lovely sheet of water, very dear to my father who was reared in these parts.

◁ Barnesmore, Donegal

One hundred and fifty years ago a traveller, the great scholar John O'Donovan, in the County of Donegal, wrote of Barnesmore from the town of Ballybofey:

Yesterday we travelled southwestwards to view that gorgeous gorge of Tirhugh, that grand and picturesque feature of Tirconnell, that memorable Gap of Danger where Patrick stood and O'Donnell fought and fell: Bearnas Mór. Its southern apex is styled Cruach Eoghanach and its northern Cruach Conallach, meaning the Kinel-Owenian and Kinel-Connellian peaks, from which it may be inferred that the southern part was anciently in Tyrone.

We climbed the steep side of Cruach Conallach to take a view of the beautiful plain lying between it and Lifford ... To the west and north the country looks mountainous and black. A remarkably level heathy plain extends far and wide to the southwest of Cruach Eoghanach in the direction of Tyrone, without the appearance of a single house or habitation of any kind. But as you look to the southwest, towards the Bay of Donegal, with the Loch of Eske receiving the waters of the Serpentine river of the Gap, a very rich district delights your eyes. To the north you see nothing but mountains.

In a century and a half the shape and make of the great Gap has not altered. People meet, the old Donegal proverb says; the mountains never.

◁ Newry, Down

Newry is Iubhar-Cinn-Tragha, the Yew Tree at the Head of the Strand, and the story is that St Patrick himself planted that yew tree. Many things have happened since then, and Newry has often been in the wars and still, alas, is.

In the centre of the town one day a Newryman said to me that we were walking on the path by which the Great O'Neill of Tyrone, opponent of the first Elizabeth of England, carried Mabel Bagenal to make her his bride. That Newryman may have been over-exercising his historical imagination, yet the romantic legend has its links with the truth. The first of the Bagenals in Ireland was, in 1552, granted by the English Crown the Lordship of Newry and Mourne, and the name long resounded in the troubled history of the North.

The town is in a hollow and the view from the Dublin-Belfast train is almost an aerial view: the Mourne Mountains and the sea to the east, and to the west the enchanted mountain of Slieve Gullion frowning down on you, and on the Gap of the North. You are sixty-five miles from Dublin and just a few miles north of that fatal Border.

Newry has suffered a lot in recent years. Why a town so strongly nationalistic and republican should be so specially selected may be hard to understand. But reason and logic on any side have not been in overwhelming evidence.

The Newry canal, no longer operative, cuts through the town, and in the distance are the Carlingford hills.

The yew tree planted by Patrick is said to have survived for seven hundred years. In 1162 it was burned, along with the adjoining monastery and all its furniture and books.

Carlingford Lough, Down ▷

High on a bald hill, above and to the north of Carlingford Lough, and above Rostrevor Forest, there's the Cloch Mór, or Great Stone, a wonderful place to be, say, on a still autumn morning. There isn't a move or a rustle on the land or a stir of breath on the polished water unless, perhaps, a small vessel might nose out of Newry and point her way across the Irish Sea towards Cumbria – and Wordsworth country. You are in County Down but can look west towards Armagh and the enchanted mountain of Slieve Gullion, and across the water to County Louth and the Cooley Hills. Somewhere on the water is The Border, hard to find as, indeed, it sometimes can be on the dry land.

An old man on this shore once said that in his youth the view was even better. He could see four kingdoms and one principality: the kingdoms of Ireland, England and Scotland, and the principality of Wales. And if he raised his heart and eyes aloft he could see the kingdom of Heaven.

△ **Warrenpoint,** Down

> You may talk of Bundoran, of Portrush and
>   Bangor,
> But come to the Point if you want to be gay.
> Yes, Billy, my boy, put your hand in your
>   pocket,
> And spend a few ha'pence and come to the say.

You will find Warrenpoint on the road from Newry town to the Mourne shore and on the northern edge of Carlingford Lough. It looks across the Narrow Water to the Cooley peninsula in County Louth and can, indeed, be a most pleasant place.

▽ **Slieve Donard and Newcastle,** Down

The top of Slieve Donard, here overlooking the seaside resort of Newcastle, County Down, is the highest place in Ulster, higher even than Mount Errigal in Donegal. Máire MacNeill writes in her great book *The Festival of Lughnasa*:

> In the eastern coast of Ireland, Slieve Donard rises even more steeply from the Irish Sea than Croagh Patrick from the Atlantic. It is the highest peak of the Mourne Mountains which stretch behind it, range upon range, to south and west, forming a massive promontory into which access by land was difficult before modern roads were made and where living was too harsh to tempt much seaborne intercourse . . .

Before the mountain came to be called Sliabh Domhanghairt, now anglicized Sliabh Donard, it was known as Sliabh Slánga. This is the name given it in the literature of the ninth to the eleventh centuries. In the last quarter of the twelfth century Giraldus Cambrensis states that Mons Dominici (the latter word obviously a misrendering of Domhangart) had replaced the older Salanga in common usage . . .

The legends surrounding the names are legion.

Domhangart, the perpetual guardian of the mountain, was said to be the son of the last pagan king of the neighbourhood, who was put in his place, or out of it, by St Patrick. Enoch Powell came later.

◁ **The Mountains of Mourne,** Down

Percy French, gentleman, of Clooneyquin in the County of Roscommon, travelled Ireland in the early part of this century in a minor official capacity, and he travelled Ireland and elsewhere as singer and reciter from the stage of his own songs and poems. He made many quiet corners radiant in his songs: Ballyjamesduff, Drumcolliher with only one street, Petravore, West Clare and its antique railway, now, alas, no more. And he paid his tribute to these dark amd mystic mountains in the song about the innocent Irish rural boy, lost amid the wonders of mighty London and remembering and longing for the place 'where dark Mourne sweeps down to the sea'.

As may be seen, the rising field pattern is something to marvel at. So is the Silent Valley in the heart of those hills.

▽ **Upper Loch Erne,** Fermanagh

The islanded beauty of Loch Erne is one of the wonders of Ireland. Fifty-seven islands, as the drunk said in the Dublin pub, one for every day in the year. They march with the great water from Killeshandra in County Cavan to the noble and historic town of Enniskillen; there the water flows under Portora where Oscar Wilde and many another went to school. The lake widens again to become Lower Lough Erne, which includes such masterpieces of islandry as Devenish and the Boa Island, and flows on to Ballyshannon, the Abbey Assaroe and the sea, inspiring the poems of William Allingham along the way:

Head out to sea when, on your lee, the breakers
  you discern.
Oh, adieu to all the billowy coasts and the
  winding banks of Erne.

Power on the Erne, Fermanagh ▷

Between Belleek in the background, and Ballyshannon, out-of-sight, and on the fringes of Counties Fermanagh and Donegal, the splendid Erne flows to meet us here in the modern world; to the benefit of electric power but not exactly to the beautifying of 'the winding banks of Erne' of William Allingham's poem. What we see is, indeed, pleasing but where the river in fine disarray used to tumble through Ballyshannon to the falls of Assaroe, it now, having accepted discipline from the Electricity Supply Board, behaves like any good canal:

Farewell to every white cascade from the
  Harbour to Belleek,
And every pool where fins may rest, and ivy-
  shaded creek,
The sloping fields, the lofty rocks, where ash and
  holly grow,
The one split yew-tree gazing on the curving
  flood below,
The lock that winds through islands under
  Turaw mountain green,
And Castle Caldwell's stretching woods with
  tranquil ways between,
And Breesie Hill, and many a pond among the
  heath and fern:
For I must say adieu, adieu to the winding banks
  of Erne.

Belleek has been famous for a long time for its craftwork in pottery and rare china, an industry set going by the Caldwells of Castle Caldwell, well up the great lake and close to Boa Island. There is a fine study of the history of that notable house, *A History of Castle Caldwell and its Families*, by John B. Cunningham (Watergate Press: Enniskillen).

Way back in pagan times Derry's name was Doire-Calgach, or the Oakgrove of Calgach. Then from Gartan in Donegal came that turbulent saint Colmcille, who founded a monastery and gave a new name to the place – Doire Cholmcille – and because of troubles at home went off to civilize the Scots. Only a tough Donegal man could have faced up to that task.

There, I feel, its name should have stayed. But later, between 1608 and 1610, the city suffered under the scheme known as the Plantation of Ulster, the systematic attempt to plant settlers there from England and Scotland in order to stabilize English government rule, and the name was changed again, to Londonderry. And after that, in 1688–9, came the Siege of Londonderry by the troops of James II, which had its own special bravery, and the long, miserable story of conflicting traditions.

This is a great city, to which we all in Ireland, from both traditions, owe much. It has had an illustrious name for music, and one of Ulster's major events was, and is, the music festival, the Feis Doire Cholmcille, and currently it has a living theatre and the presence of one of Ireland's finest playwrights, Brian Friel.

As a schoolboy I performed in a plainchant choir on the Guildhall stage, and walked the old walls, and studied the great gun, Roaring Meg, and the marks of the knees of Colmcille on a stone in the Long Church Tower.

◁ **Grianan of Aileach,** Donegal

'Said Shiela Ni Gara, " 'Tis a kind wind and true,
   For it rustled oft through Aileach's halls and
      stirred the hair of Hugh"'...

Ethna Carberry's poem relates to the legend that there on Greenan Hill, under the circular stone fort of the Grianan, or sunhouse, of the territory of Aileach, the great Hugh O'Neill, who never died, sits with his men in a faery sleep and waits for the moment of awakening and the liberation of Ireland, *Lá ar bith feasa*: Any day now.

This most impressive circular structure was in ancient time the fortress of the O'Neills. Over the centuries the fort has suffered both from the destruction of war and the zeal of restorers. But it is still majestic and commands a vast prospect over the place where Derry and Donegal together meet the salt water.

◁ **Coleraine,** Londonderry

Of all Irish rivers, the Bann is the greatest survivor. It emerges somewhere away at the back of the Mourne country and flows through Bannbridge, about which one of the loveliest of Irish love songs has been written. It lives through an encounter with Portadown, enters Lough Neagh, and emerges from that waste of waters at Toomebridge and Portglenone to go on to meet the sea at the town of Coleraine – a curious and colourless town created and much favoured by English planters in the early seventeenth century. For not quite creditable and political reasons it now has a university. But its chief claim to fame is in a song 'Kitty of Coleraine', written by an eighteenth-century character by the name of Pleasant Ned Lysaght:

> As beautiful Kitty one morning was
>   tripping, with
> A pitcher of milk from the fair of
>   Coleraine,
> When she saw me she stumbled,
> The pitcher down tumbled.
> And all the sweet buttermilk watered
>   the plain.

◁ **Mussenden House,** Downhill, Londonderry

Indeed there is in this country but one opinion concerning that nobleman – that he is the most accomplished gentleman, the most learned scholar, the warmest friend, the most charitable prelate, the most liberal ecclesiastic, and the most humane man we have ever seen – With regard to your imputation on him, it seems to lie in a very small compass: either the lady, whom you suppose him base enough to seduce, corresponded with his love, or she did not. If she did, how came you to know what nobody heard or believes of a most virtuous, chaste and innocent lady? If she did not – then, she herself may hold this relation and seducer in the utmost abhorrence. Now it is well known that she holds him in the utmost esteem, reverence and affection, that her husband allows her still to receive such presents from her noble relation, (which by the bye is no less than a first cousin once removed), as suits the generosity of his mind, and the tenderness of his affection . . .

So a most indignant inhabitant of Lisburne wrote, in 1783, to the Dublin *Volunteer Evening Post* to refute scandalous charges made against the celebrated Bishop of Derry and Earl of Bristol, Frederick Hervey, and his lovely cousin, Mrs Mussenden.

In 1780 Hervey had John Adam build this house for him on the extreme northern sea coast, close to Coleraine and the little resort of Castlerock. It was destroyed by fire in 1803. The speck on the cliff edge is an ornamental temple, perhaps a love-bower, for the fascinating cousin. Who are we to judge?

39

Lough Muckno, Monaghan

In a public house in the town of Castleblayney in the County Monaghan, and thirty or more years ago, I heard the publican sing, at my request, the beautiful ballad of the Maid of Lord Blayney's demesne, about which ballad I had, up to that moment, only heard rumours:

When the foes all surround me in battle,
And I'm in the midst of all pain,
To you I'll be true, lovely Mary,
Fair maid of Lord Blayney's demesne.

We are looking down now on a portion of what was Lord Blayney's demesne, and on the lovely Lough Muckno, a hidden masterpiece.

A Sir Edward Blayney built a castle here and was governor of the County of Monaghan under that careful man and wisest fool in Christendom, James I. And Blayney is still a strong name in the North.

The River Fane more-or-less takes its origin in that lake and flows eastward to the Irish Sea, through the village of Inniskeen.

Monaghan town withdrawn in the clouds – but for the high spire of St Macartan's Cathedral. This was the town in which Charles Gavan Duffy, founder with John Mitchel and Thomas Davis of the newspaper *The Nation* was born, and in which there is a famous college for young men and an even more famous school, run by the Louis nuns, for young women.

Below the clouds are clean, quiet streets and some fine eighteenth-century buildings and a pub where you may rest when the Derry Express halts for a while on the way north from Dublin to Omagh.

And one of the finest of Ulster ballads, in English, begins with a reference to Monaghan town – the tuneful story of the Inniskilling Dragoon:

A beautiful damsel of fame and renown,
A gentleman's daughter from Monaghan town,
As she drove by the barracks, this beautiful maid
Stood up in her carriage to see the parade.

△ **Lifford and Strabane,** Donegal and Tyrone

Where the Finn River (on the right), coming from the long and lovely Lough Finn in the heart of the Donegal highlands, meets the Mourne Water from County Tyrone to form the Foyle (on the left), are the towns of Lifford (in the foreground) and Strabane. The big bridge that joins them is one of the chief gateways to the wonders of Donegal. The unfortunate Border that separates them has meant that Strabane has been exposed to more than its share of the irrationalities of our time, even to an attempt at aerial bombardment.

Perhaps the towns are best known through a lovely song:

But farewell till bonny Lifford where the sweet
 Mourne waters flow,
And likewise until my brownhaired girl, since I
 from her must go.
As down Lough Foyle the waters boil, and my
 ship stands out from the land,
I'll say farewell and God bless you, my flower
 sweet Strabane.

There is also the song about Moorlough Mary whose lover first glimpsed her at the market of sweet Strabane, where 'the hearts of all men she did trepann'.

Some notable names can be traced back to this river-crossing: Captain John Dunlap (1747–1812), apprentice printer in Strabane, who emigrated and lived to print the first copies of the American Declaration of Independence; James Wilson, another printer, and the grandfather of President Woodrow Wilson; Dr George Sigerson, professor of Biology in Dublin, poet, scholar, very proud of his Viking origins, and the author of, among other books, the invaluable *Bards of the Gael and Gall*. And, in our own time, Flann O'Brien or Myles na Goppaleen, or to give him his name from the font, Brian O'Nolan.

△ **Sion Mills,** Tyrone

The river is the Mourne: the Big River. It becomes the Mourne where the Owenkillew from the Sperrin mountains joins the Strule at Newtownstewart in the County Tyrone. Still happy in Tyrone, it flows north to Strabane to be joined by the Finn from the heart of Donegal, and to become the Foyle.

The Herdman family founded and have for long managed these prosperous mills. The name Sion has nothing to do with the biblical original, nor with that happy land to which we are all bound, but is superimposed on the original Irish, Suidhe Fhinn, or the camping-place of Fionn.

Sweet Omagh Town, Tyrone ▷

Thrice happy and blessed were the days of my
   childhood
And happy the hours I wandered from school
By Mountjoy's green forest, our dear native
   wildwood,
And the green flowery banks of the serpentine
   Strule.

We look down on the handsome town I was reared in, so I hope the personal note may be forgiven. But the lines quoted were not, alas, written by me. They come, with no credit title that I have ever heard of, out of the shadows of the early nineteenth century.

Northward and downstream, and on the horizon in this picture, are the old estates of Lord Mountjoy, the Earl of Blessington. The great lady herself did once, only, visit the place. The timber trade was good when Napoleon was at his best or worst and the Blessington forest rangers did the felling. But after Waterloo came the slump and the emigration of the woodsmen, many of them Irish-speakers, to Quebec and beyond. That quotation was the first verse of a lament for their passing.

In the bottom right-hand corner of the picture the Camowen River, coming from the right, joins the Drumragh (more exactly, the Owenreagh) to form the Strule, which flows northward to become the Mourne, or the Big River, at Newtownstewart, and then the Foyle from Derry to the sea. Parallel to the Strule, the Market Street and the High Street run up to the fine classical courthouse, and to the soaring spires of the Catholic Church and the Church of Ireland. Sir Tyrone Guthrie once said that if somebody tilted the High Street the other way for him, so as to seat an audience, he could direct a fine passion play on the courthouse steps.

King James II and his entourage passed that way on their road to the fatal walls of Derry, and made a one-night stand in the town.

From proud Dungannon to Ballyshannon,
From Cullyhanna to old Ardboe,
I've roamed and rambled, caroused and
   gambled,
Where song did thunder and whiskey flow.
It's light and airy I roamed through Derry
Or to Portaferry in the County Down.
But with all my raking and undertaking,
My heart was aching for sweet Omagh town.

44

Munster

In that enormous castle on the left bank of the Shannon you may now be entertained at a medieval banquet and listen to the Bunratty singers, and if you transgress the rules of the banquet, which are a little difficult to define, you may even be, briefly and in a most friendly fashion, confined in an ancient dungeon. At any rate that was the way it was in the early days of the Bunratty banquets, when you might also drink mead, or a liquid substance so described, and which tasted quite good.

You are eight miles from Limerick city and on the road to Shannon Airport, under whose guiding wings the banquet proceeds. The adjacent river, the Ratty or Owenagarney, is a very minor part of the Shannon system.

The history of a fortification at that river-crossing goes back over seven hundred years, but the present structure dates probably from the mid-fifteenth century. It was a castle of the O'Briens but, like many such places, frequently changed hands. Under the Parliament in 1645 it was held for a while by Admiral William Penn, father of that William who gave his name to Pennsylvania; and before the castle became a tourist attraction it was the property of Lord Gort.

◁ **Caherconnell,** Clare

The distinctive stone ring-fort of Caherconnell grows out of the limestone plateau of the Burren in County Clare. The ring-forts were farm settlements of pre-Christian and early Christian times, and Caherconnell sits beside its modern counterpart, a snug County Clare farmstead.

Caherconnell lies in the north of the Kilcorney Valley, which has many of the other features of the Burren – ancient field patterns, limestone caves, fugitive lakes called 'turloughs' and Stone Age gallery tombs.

The late Sir John Betjeman caught the spirit of the strange lunar landscape in his poem 'Ireland with Emily':

Stony seaboard far and foreign
Stony hills formed over space
Stony outcrop of the Burren
Stones in every fertile place
Little fields with boulders dotted
Grey-stone shoulders saffron-spotted.
Stone-walled cabins thatched with reeds
Where a Stone Age people breeds,
The last of Europe's stone age race.

◁ Cliffs of Moher, Clare

County Clare has always presented a bold face to the Atlantic and whatever lies beyond it, and the Cliffs of Moher seen from the air, the land or from the sea are never anything but awesome. If you step over the edge you could drop, say, six hundred feet before you hit the water. So do not walk there on a windy day. The seagulls, flying and screaming halfway down, when seen from above, seem motionless. There are also wild goats in the neighbourhood.

Away to the left are the village and holy well of Liscannor. And there is a monument to a Cornelius O'Brien MP, erected by himself to himself and, it is said, his tenants paid the cost. It is also said that he had the monument raised to celebrate the achievement of his century in children born out of wedlock. A man in the neighbouring town of Lahinch told me that. But they're great storytellers in Lahinch.

The Burren, Clare ▷

Cromwell's General Ludlow, riding into the Burren of north Clare, declared that the strange green-and-white land had not water enough to drown a man, timber enough to hang him, or earth enough to bury him. Or words to that effect. The General may not have been interested in either geology or botany: and for geologists and botanists the Burren (the Rock) is a unique place. When the flowering time comes, the rarest blossoms shine in the very crevices of the stones; and among the rocks, and in beautiful little green valleys, the wild goats brood. It is a strange experience to walk there alone in the dusk. Faraway the white rocks seem to move. The goats are motionless.

Also in younger years I covered a lot of it on foot, and in daylight, with Sean J. White who is an enthusiast and authority. Bad country for broken ankles.

The antiquarian treasures are plentiful. For me the gem is the ruin of the ancient abbey of Corcomroe which W.B. Yeats imaginatively used as the setting for his play 'The Dreaming of the Bones'. It heightens the appreciation of the moonscape of the Burren to read these lines from the beginning of that play:

Somewhere among great rocks, on the scarce
    grass,
Birds cry, then cry their loneliness.
Even the sunlight can be lonely here,
Even hot noon is lonely.

The French, with Theobold Wolfe Tone (source of the idea of the Irish republic) on board, sailed into Bantry Bay in 1798 and came so close to landing that you could have tossed a coin ashore. But the weather was rough and that landing was never made. Over the centuries British warships marked these wide waters, and in the First World War a contingent took off for the Battle of Jutland. And, according to the song, the little herring fleet at anchor lay at the old stone quay, and every lassie to her sailor-lad was saying: 'You're welcome back to Bantry Bay.'

And the modern world came here to Whiddy Island, and the long tankers, to be followed, as the night the day, by a most unfortunate disaster. A tanker caught fire and several were killed. Whiddy Island has most assuredly been pock-marked by the craving and crying-out of the western world for Arabian oil.

△ **Lisdoonvarna,** Clare

The springs of Lisdoonvarna in the County Clare have sulphur and chalybeate elements which are reputed to be good for your ailment or complaint if it is of an arthritic or rheumatic nature. But, like most resorts from Bath to Ballybunion (or Loch Derg), Lisdoon over the years developed a second reputation as a meeting place for aspiring bachelors and wistful maidens. Nobody can deny that when they come together there in the holiday season Lisdoon is one of the most colourful places in Ireland.

Along with Lahinch, Enistymon and Ballyvaughan, it is a convenient starting point for an exploration of the Clare coast and the quite unique area of the Burren of north Clare. The nearest big centres are the town of Ennis in one direction and Galway city in the other.

▽ Blarney Castle, Cork

The groves of Blarney, they look so charming
All by the purlings of sweet silent brooks,
All decked with posies that spontaneous grow
   there,
Planted in order in the rocky nooks.
'Tis there the daisy and the sweet carnation,
The blooming pink and the rose so fair,
Likewise the lily and the daffodilly,
All flowers that scent the sweet open air.

So to praise the beauties of Blarney, and that wondrous stone in Blarney Castle, that can give speech to the dumb, I call the songwriter out of the shadows of almost two centuries. The song is attributed to Millikin:

There are statues gracing this noble place in
All heathen gods and nymphs so fair,
Bold Neptune, Caesar and Nebuchadnezzar
All standing naked in the open air . . .
There is a stone there that whoever kisses,
Oh! he never misses to grow eloquent,
'Tis he may clamber to a lady's chamber
Or become a member of parliament.
A clever spouter he'll sure turn out, or
An out-and-outer to be let alone.
Don't hope to hinder him or to bewilder him,
Sure he's a pilgrim from the Blarney Stone.

Blarney's massive four-storey keep was probably the work of Cormac Laidir MacCarthy of Muskerry in 1446 and his descendants held on to the castle, with a few interruptions, until 1690, when Cork fell to the Williamites.

The origin of 'blarney', meaning to placate with soft talk or to smoothly flatter, is said to lie in the stream of unfulfilled promises of Cormac MacDermot MacCarthy, chatelain of Blarney around 1600. Having promised to deliver his castle to Carew, Lord President of Munster under Elizabeth I, he endlessly put off the day, soothing him with persuasive talk, which came to be known as 'blarney'.

Skibbereen, Cork ▷

West Cork is a world in itself, and a great part of the charm of West Cork, not forgetting the splendour of inlet and headland, is in its small towns, tucked away, you might say, in nooks and corners. There is Skibbereen, on the River Ilen, and there are Clonakilty and Ballydehob and Baltimore and Dunmanway and Glandore and Castletownshend and more. They are distinct and proud and self-centred, yet most welcoming to strangers.

There is a story that a man from Skibbereen went all the way to Cork city to join one of those mystery tours about which he had heard so much, and the touring-bus brought him back to Skibbereen. Which convinced him quite rightly, if he had not already guessed it, that his town was the centre of the universe. That story I have also heard told about Clonakilty.

Skibbereen has a fine early nineteenth-century classical-style Cathedral; and is much sung about in a famous ballad about the sad times of famine, evictions of the poor and emigration.

On Sunday, the 28th of May, 1848, he landed at Cove [Cobh], and was rowed in a boat to the prison of Spike Island. Having been handed over to the Governor he was conducted to a vaulted chamber which was to be his cell, and here, as soon as he was alone, his pent-up feelings gave way, and he burst into a flood of passionate tears. These were not tears of base lamentation for his fate – but tears of regret and pity for his country … In a short time he recovered himself and, standing up, exclaimed: 'I am ready for my fourteen years ordeal, and whether it bring me toil, sickness, ignominy or death – fate, thou art defied.'

That passage was written about John Mitchel, who was sentenced to transportation to the penal colonies for fourteen years for defying government or misgovernment and for a crime then newly described as treason-felony. Over its long years in British hands and its briefer period, so far, in Irish hands, the island has had many transients. Of late it has been transformed into a retreat house for youthful, urban joy-riders or fall guys. A few of them have shown their appreciation by attempting to joy ride on rafts back to Mother Érin. Their true opinion of Spike has not yet been more elaborately expressed. Unlike John Mitchel, none of them has yet written a Jail Journal.

The whole fate of Ireland, Professor Edmund Curtis wrote in his *A History of Ireland*, hung upon a single battle – in the days around Christmas of 1601.

A victory for O'Neill would have led to further aid from Spain and a great flocking to his standard, for Mountjoy himself records how much of the population, even the Old English, had 'Spanish and Papist hearts', and that 'in the cities of Munster' the citizens were so degenerated from their first English progenitors as that the very speaking of English was forbidden by them to their wives and children …

Everything favoured O'Neill's Fabian tactics for, by wastage, on Dec. 2, the Deputy [Mountjoy] had only 6,500 men fit for arms, while Tyrone had 6,000 foot and 500 horse, with 3,000 Spaniards inside Kinsale. But the Spaniards pressed for a decisive battle … in which through mismanagement the combination of Spaniards and Irish failed, and O'Neill, who favoured waiting for another day, was forced into action by O'Donnell, which ended in a rout for the Irish. In this the losses of the Irish were reckoned from 1,000 to 2,000, among whom a Spanish squadron on the Irish side, and 840 out of 900 Scots, under MacDonnell captains, were slain outright.

Such was the sudden and astonishing termination of a long war in which the Irish had gained victory after victory. O'Donnell in terrible agitation took ship for Spain, where next year he died in Salamanca, with the suspicion that an English agent poisoned him. O'Neill marched back to the north, while D'Aguila shamefully surrendered without making any terms for his Irish confederates …

Because the Old Head of Kinsale reached out so far towards Spain, this place was for a long time a sensitive spot in the defences of English power; so it was solidly fortified against invasion from the sea. That danger to England passed, and also the threat from France, but some amazing fortifications remain, in a state, naturally enough, of decrepitude. Of those two star-shaped structures, the more massive is Charles Fort, on the right of the picture called after Charles II. British troops were in the fort until 1922, and after the evacuation it was burned by Republican irregulars – what of it would burn. It is still an awesome structure. And on the promontory of Ringrone to the left is James Fort, built in 1601 to the design of Paul Ive and called after the other James, the wisest fool in Christendom.

◁ Cork Beside the Lee, Cork

This vision is best left to the description of a Corkman:

> Leaving us, the summer visitor says in his good-humoured way that Cork is quite a busy place, considering how small it is. And he really thinks so, because whatever little we have of pastors, postmen, urchins, beggars, of squares, streets, lanes, markets, of wagons, motors, tramcars, ships, of spires, turrets, domes, towers, of bells, horns, meetings, cries, concert-halls, theatres, shops, are flung higgledy-piggledy together into a narrow, double-streamed, many-bridged river valley, jostled and jostling, so compacted that the mass throws up a froth and flurry that confuses the stray visitor, unless indeed he is set on getting at the true size and worth of things. For him this is Cork. But for us it is only the Flat of the City. What of the hillsides? Go but three steps up any of those old-time, wide-sweeping, treeless, cloud-shadowed hills and you find yourself even at midday in a silence that grows on you. You have scarce left the city yet you raise your eyes, you look around and notice little gable ends that finish in little crosses of stone or arched gateways of sandstone or limestone or both, or far-stretching garden walls that are marked with tablets of brass on which are cut holy emblems and sacred letters – and as you look the silence seems to grow deeper and deeper: indeed you have come on the very fruitage of the spirit of contemplation – convents, monasteries, chapels, hospitals, houses of refuge. And to us these quiet hillsides also are Cork.

That was Daniel Corkery, one of the great Cork writers of this century. For further descriptions of Cork beside the Lee, see the works of Sean O'Faolain, Frank O'Connor and others. And there are many songs, onwards from Francis Sylvester Mahony and the Bells of Shandon. Or for word of mouth go to Jack Lynch, former Taoiseach and famous sportsman, or to Joe Lynch, actor, singer, man of fun and wisdom ...

Granted, Corkery wrote that sixty-seven years ago and Cork has altered and grown a lot since then, but the passage is still true to the living, humorous, meditative spirit of the place, which had its monastic beginnings in the sixth to seventh century with St Finbar. Since then a lot of people have passed through a place that turns a humpy back on Ireland and faces out to Europe and the open ocean.

Cork City, Cork

The River Lee is seen here with one of its arms engaged in what Edmund Spenser described as enclosing Cork 'with its divided flood'. The city, like Venice, rose from a series of islands in a flat marsh but, unlike Venice, can be viewed from surrounding sentinel hills. The 'flat' of the city is its old commercial and civic centre. South Mall, the gracious, classical street running diagonally across the top of the picture, was once a channel or canal with merchants' houses and boats tied to the high front steps. The wedding cake gothic fantasy in the centre of Holy Trinity Church façade is a successful and sprightly addition to the regency-gothic church designed by George Richard Pain for the famous Capuchin temperance reformer Father Theobald Matthew. Father Matthew's statue stands in Cork's main street to commemorate his valiant (but unsuccessful) effort to make Ireland sober.

◁ **Magillicuddy's Reeks,** Kerry

Just from here it does not look like the highest point of Ireland of the Welcomes but in all truth, it is. This is what winter looks like on Magillicuddy's Reeks, the high, mountainous heart of the Kingdom of Kerry. On the top of Carrauntoohil, at 3,414 feet above the sea, you are as high as an Irishman may rise in his own country. Most of us may find it more comforting to look up to it on a summer day, from Glenbeigh or Lough Acoose or Glencar.

▽ **Ross Castle,** Loch Leane, Kerry

Forty-one years ago, in the autumn, I made my first meditation on Ross Castle on the shore of Loch Leane:

The tourists jolt on sidecars through the Muckross estate, hear jokes and fables prepared for their predecessors in the dawn of tourism, pay their money to view the lakes, pay more money and view the Torc waterfall. The same sidecars, the same jarveys, ponies and a similar strain of anecdote carry them up the gloomy gap of Dunloe, abandon them to boats and boatmen and the cool enchantment of the lakes, the excitement of the rapids, the landing under the shadow of Ross Castle. More money and they may climb the tower, uncomfortably conscious of

the chill in the wind, the lack of summer light in the wide tossing water on the great walls of the mountains. When the last echo of their steps has gone from the dull walls and the twisting stairway, the darkness, the mists from lake and mountain can thicken around the castle … lulling and deluding the mind, making every noise the rattle of a horse hoof, the slap of a scabbard, every glimmer of lost light on a stone or a wet leaf like the abrupt flash of steel. The wooded places by the lake might be alive with men, presences that have never left the place, Ludlow's Cromwellians who closed around and captured this castle, trampled on this soil and on these stones, trampled also on a separate civilization, on a distinct way of life …

▽ The Great Blasket, Kerry

The boat runs rapidly over the waves to the hasty rhythm of the six short, almost bladeless oars: or, if the wind is fair, following the pull of the tiny, patched sail. You see the coast going by, and the blunt headland of Dún Mór, once the home of a fabled goddess, with a rock at its end – An Sean duine, the old man, a familiar seamark to the islanders. Then the lifting prow turns to the Islands, and in a short while the boat is running by Beginis, and the high front of the island begins to rise over you. To the right is a long shore of sand, An Iráigh Bhán, the white strand, and in front a flat reef of rock, anvil-shaped, shuts in the tiny harbour. The boat runs in, turns on its axis, and you are floating easily up to the ship, under a great cliff fringed with the children perilously running on its dizzy brink . . .

The children no longer run on that dizzy brink. For the living people have left the Great Blasket in the ultimate south-west and its subsidiary islands: with the exception of a notable political figure who has a summer place on Inish Vicillaune. And at the moment of writing there have been hints that the Great Blasket may end up as a holiday camp, hints that have not been and should not be too well received.

What I have just been quoting was how it seemed to Robin Flower, Englishman and Celtic scholar, when he first came there in 1910. His classical book *The Western Island, or, The Great Blasket* was published in 1944.

That now lost and lonely island gave us some of the classics of modern literature in Irish: Tomás Ó Crohan's *The Islandman*, her own story, *Peig*, by Peig Sayers and Maurice O'Sullivan's, *Twenty Years A-growing*.

The greatest living authority on the story of the island would be Bryan MacMahon, novelist, playwright and master of the short story.

Killarney, Kerry ▷

In autumn the red and brown of the mountains colour the cooling air. You can leave Killarney behind you, walk along the road with the grey wall that hides the beauties of Muckross on your right hand, and the moving shoulder of Torc above you on the left, up and up until everything touristed and ticketed is below in the deep valley . . . until the silence of the high places has seeped into your soul.

The last few lingering tourists . . . circle obediently on the Ring of Kerry, down the Laune to Killorglin, up the steep street, out over level moorland until the great stretch of Dingle Bay is visible from the high road under the shadow of Drung Hill . . .

That was myself forty-one years ago, having my first look at Killarney, and the mountains, lakes, rivers and coasts of Kerry, and beginning a long article for Fr Senan's *Capuchin Annual*, on Aogán Ó Rathaille. He was the greatest of the Kerry poets of the eighteenth-century, and the greatest Irish poet before Yeats – according to Thomas Kinsella and others who speak with authority. One of the chief ornaments of Killarney town is the monument to those Kerry poets by the sculptor Seamus Murphy. There is also the fine cathedral by Augustus Welby Pugin.

And the town is the chief gateway to all the scenic wonders of that part of the world, appreciated by everyone from Charles James Fox to Boucicault and Benedict, from Thackeray to Daniel O'Connell and that American gentleman who wrote 'Home, Sweet Home'. But the spirit of the town is best captured in the short stories of Seamus De Faoite.

Innisfallen, Kerry

One morning early as I walked out on the
    margin of Loch Leane,
The sunshine dressed the trees in green and
    summer bloomed again …

The songs about Killarney and its lakes are many,
nor would I have the termerity to quote the one
about the lakes and fells, emerald isles and winding
bays, mountain paths and woodland dells where
memory ever fondly strays; nor about how the
angels fold their wings and rest in that Eden of the
West. For the angels I cannot answer but the truth
is that no song, however wild in hyperbole, could do
justice to the beauty of the lakes and the land
around them and the islands on them: and Inisfallen, seen here when the leaves were no longer
green, is, at any time of the year, one of the gems.

The ruin is of a Romaneque church and the
island was the site of St Fionán Lobhar's monastery,
founded in the sixth–seventh century. Six hundred
or so years later the monks accepted the Augustinian rule.

The Annals of Inisfallen are in the Bodleian
Library, Oxford, and the Inisfallen Crozier, found in
the River Leane in 1867, is to be seen in the
National Museum in Kildare Street, Dublin.

The lines quoted above are from 'The Dawning of
the Day', a song popularized in a celebrated record-
ing by John McCormack.

62

△ **Aughinish Island,** Limerick

Oh, Limerick it is beautiful, as everybody knows.
The River Shannon, full of fish, beside that city
    flows . . .

Everybody does, indeed, know, and the 'spacious Shenan, spreading like a sea', as Edmund Spenser saw it, would offset any city, especially a city that possesses one of the finest main streets in Ireland – O'Connell Street – and the Georgian Crescent; the impressive remains of King John's Castle, dominating Thomond Bridge and eight hundred years old; a famous rowing club; and it is commonly said, the handsomest women in Ireland.

The river, of course, made the city and brought with it a tumultuous procession of tidal waves of history. Green valleys, according to Seneca, never feel the force of thunder, but to live at a country's most important crossroads and river-crossing never could make for peace.

The river brought the marauding Vikings, who went far upstream beyond where Limerick now stands. But in about 922 they made a settlement at this spot and so began Ireland's fourth largest city. Battles and sieges, meetings and counter-meetings followed over the centuries. Brian Boru reduced the place to ashes in 967. The Normans stormed it in 1175. Edward the Bruce, brother of Robert, took it in 1315. Cromwell's son-in-law, Henry Ireton did the same in 1651. William of Orange tried to take it but, in a celebrated event of 1691, Patrick Sarsfield, the Jacobite commander, stole out from the city and destroyed the Williamite siege train at Ballyneety. The Williamites returned and captured Limerick, and on a tragic and historic stone in the castle the treaty of surrender was signed, and broken. Two fine twin-towered gatehouses and some of the walls survive to prove how stoutly the city could have been, and was, defended.

The River Shannon, 'spreading like a sea' as Edmund Spenser describes it, has many wonders on its banks and on its estuary islands. There are castles like the toyland eighteenth-century castle in which lives the Knight of Glin; old battered fortresses like Carrigogunnell and Askeaton, gracious classic houses like Shannongrove and Tarbert.

There are also modern 'wonders' like this aluminium plant on Aughinish Island, which is spreading its red stain on the landscape, though not, one hopes, in the surrounding waters.

Right beside Aughinish is the little port of Foynes, where the first trans-Atlantic commercial airships made their European landfall in 1939. Nowadays, just across the estuary from Aughinish Island, lies Shannon Airport.

Romantic Ireland's dead and gone,
It's with O'Leary in the grave ...

And the O'Leary that the poet Yeats mourned in the early years of this century was John O'Leary (1830–1907), one of the supreme Fenian revolutionaries and a man of such high honour that he considered there were things a man should not do, not even to save his own country. Times have changed in Ireland and elsewhere and the meaning of salvation has been somewhat obscured.

O'Leary, who so inspired the young Yeats, was a native of Tipperary town; and, as Lord Killanin and Professor Duignan remind us, the father of Eugene O'Neill came from the neighbourhood, as did that stern and sensible critic William Hazlitt, and also blind Liam O'Hilfearnain, notable Gaelic poet of the eighteenth century.

Tipperary town has other claims to distinction. To mention two: people of my own surname are as plentiful as blackberries in that part of the world, and if you leave the town slowly, and go in the right direction, and rise and rise, you will come to a place where, all of a sudden, you look down on the wonder of the Glen of Aherlow.

△ **Ballyporeen,** Tipperary

President Reagan was happy to find that his people came from Ballyporeen in the County Tipperary. A pleasant little town under the handsome shadow of the Knockmealdown Mountains. And the people of Ballyporeen were happy to welcome President Reagan.

Unlike (in the song) Donnegan's daughter from over the water, he created no slaughter in Ballyporeen.

◁ Cashel, Tipperary

A poet could well see visions on the Rock of Cashel. Yeats did:

On the grey rock of Cashel the mind's eye
Has called up the cold spirits . . .

Cold chapel, the most part of a thousand years old, arched empty windows, ancient tombs, crabbed symbolic carvings, tall tower, tiny stone heads that look out of dark corners with eyes that seem curiously alive.

Then out into the sunlight and the vision of flat, fertile, riverine land limited by the high Galtys to the south-west, the most graceful of Ireland's mountain ranges:

On the grey Rock of Cashel I suddenly saw
A sphinx with woman breast and lion paw,
A Buddha, hand at rest,
Hand lifted up that blest.

The images cut in stone in Cashel, the beast with the trefoil tail, the centaur shooting a lion with a bow and arrow, were certainly capable of inspiring in Yeats that difficult poem. For the Rock itself, from land or air, is a vision. No one will ever forget his first prospect of the Rock of Cashel.

There was a time, perhaps, when the outline of man's work on the Rock was simpler, when Cormac's chapel, the twelfth-century gem of the place (in fact, a small, exquisite Romanesque cathedral built at the wish of Cormac MacCarthy, King of Desmond), would have been clearly visible from a distance and the traveller approaching could have thought in the terms used by a scholar of the last century, the great Dr Murray of Maynooth:

But to make thee, of loving hearts the love
Was coined to living stone.
Truth, peace and piety together strove
To form thee for their own.

A light, when darkness on the nations dwelt,
In Erin found a home.
The mind of Greece, the warm heart of the Celt,
The bravery of Rome.

◁ Monahincha, Tipperary

There was a lake here once, Loch Cré, a mile or so away from the town of Roscrea. The lake was drained the best part of three centuries ago and it became possible to go on foot, even if stumbling over a causeway or squelching over Monahincha bog, on to Inis mBeó, Insula Viventium, the Island of the Living. There was a small monastery here associated with the mysterious and austere Culdee (Célé Dé), and dedicated to the Virgin who was the only lady allowed next or near the place. For tradition has it that monastic seclusion was so strict that no female of any species was tolerated on the Inis, or Inch.

There was also an ancient belief that the dead buried down there could not decay. Hence perhaps the colourful and resounding name – although one must not be unmindful of the spiritual connotation.

It is a good place to pause and meditate before you enter St Cronan's Roscrea, rich in memorials of the monastic past.

The Knockmealdown Mountains, Waterford ▷

All night around the thorn tree the Little People
  play,
And men and women passing will turn their
  head away . . .

Little People cry out for capital letters lest they treat
us roughly for disrespect.

A lady novelist, Temple Lane, whom I had the
privilege of meeting, wrote that winsome song
about the village of Clogheen at the foot of the
Knockmealdown Mountains, say fourteen miles
from the town of Clonmel, through which George
Borrow and Oliver Cromwell and Black Hugh
O'Neill, and myself, and several others, passed.

The song was beautifully sung by a singer whom
I was also privileged to know. His name was John
MacCormack:

And if your heart's a child's heart, and if your
  eyes are clean,
You'll never fear the thorntree that grows
  beyond Clogheen.

And above Clogheen rise Knockshanahullion and
Sugarloaf Hill, the highest of the Knockmealdown
Mountains, and through them runs this crazy road.
They call it the Vee. Since a little after Walter Scott
and Wordsworth, and since the days of improved
road transport, all romantics have loved mountain
passes. This is one of the most impressive mountain
passes in Ireland.

△ Athassel Priory, Tipperary

Athassel Abbey, as it is commonly called, is but a
few miles away from Cashel and close to the
attractive and happily named village of Golden, on
the sweet banks of the River Suir, about which there
are more haunting songs than I have time to talk
about. It is more properly described as a priory, an
Augustinian establishment, set there in the twelfth
century by the Norman William de Burgo and
dedicated to St Edmund, martyr King of East Anglia.
Even the English saints had the colonizing impulse.

▽ The Nore and the Barrow

Roundabout where the Leinster counties of Wexford and Kilkenny meet, the rivers Nore and Barrow also have their confluence. It is one of the most impressive meetings-of-the-waters in Ireland. Standish O'Grady wrote of the Nore at this meeting place as a novice and of the Barrow as an abbess. The image is not inexact even if the Nore, on its way down from the Slieve Bloom mountains, has burdened itself with all the history of Kilkenny and that rich Norman land. The Barrow emerges from those same mountains, sweeps through Kildare and Carlow and by ancient Graignamanagh, in County Kilkenny. Meeting here, they go on by New Ross to join the Suir, from Waterford, and the sea.

◁ Vincent O'Brien's Stud Farm, Tipperary

The horse on which Miss Kilmansegg with the golden leg (in Thomas Hood's famous poem) rode, and got run away with in Hyde Park, had to be, because of her high notions, an Irish thoroughbred and could only have come from such opulent Tipperary land as that which we see in the picture.

At first sight from above it might seem to be an airfield. But no: not airplanes but some of the greatest horses of this or any century have taken off from that ground and from the tutelage of the most celebrated Vincent O'Brien.

Patrick Kavanagh, the poet, said in the presence of two reliable witnesses that there never had been a properly-canonized Irish saint because nobody had ever performed the three attested miracles; but the one man eligible would be Vincent O'Brien because of three Champion Hurdles in a row, three gold cups in a row, and three Nationals in a row.

We see here the nineteenth-century marvel, or monstrosity, according to your predilections, of Lismore Castle, frowning o'er the Blackwater, the most Rhinelike of our rivers. That stupendous castle dominates and devours the handsome town of Lismore. Or so I always feel when I pass that way.

Lismore has a long history of castles, back to Henry II and the incorrigible Prince John, and taking in Sir Walter Raleigh, who sold the castle and estates in 1602 to Richard Boyle, Earl of Cork, and a remarkable Elizabethan adventurer, and going on to those always-with-us wars of the Confederation and of Cromwell. In the mid-eighteenth century the place became the property of the Duke of Devonshire. In 1812 Lady Caroline Lamb came here to stay with her cousin, the sixth Duke, to help her to forget Byron; she was bitterly disappointed by the castle's opulence and comfort, having expected 'vast apartments full of tattered furniture and gloom'. Adele Astaire, who married a Cavendish, lived here for a while.

By contrast: in 1814 the Lismore Crozier, now in the National Museum, and what is now known as the Book of Lismore were found in a hole in a wall of the castle. The Book is a most valuable collection of the lives of the saints and other matters – a fifteenth-century monastic compilation.

Spenser celebrated the Blackwater as he did so many Irish and English rivers, with the settled idea that all rivers were tributaries of Sweete Thames.

Tramore, meaning Big Strand, is much frequented by Munster and Leinster people seeking sun and salt water. For horsemen and others there are always Tramore Races, but the cliff walks along the bold County Waterford coastline can be particularly inspiriting.

These three columns, built in the early nineteenth century as navigation marks, provide one of the sights as the terminating point, on Great Newton Head, of one of those walks. In the middle is the Metal Man, a mariner dressed in the uniform of Nelson's day.

Local tradition has it that any unmarried girl who can hop all the way round the Metal Man's column will wed within the year.

◁ **Waterford City,** Waterford

Here comes [to the quays of Waterford] the Welsh harbinger of woe, Geraldus Cambrensis, who drew that picture of Waterford as a conquered city, which induced Henry II to land, with all his legions, at Waterford in 1171, the first English King to set foot in Ireland ... The city's ruler [at the time], the Dane who built the Tower, Reginald MacGillemory, who endeavoured to ambush the royal fleet [bearing five thousand men at arms] by stretching a chain across the Suir below the city, was captured by the English. This, the first prisoner of war brought before an English King in Ireland, was hanged. All honour to the memory of this Gaelicised Dane ...

And when Henry was gone ... came his son, Prince John, the execrated, who found a secure repose here, and even built himself a castle and pleasure-grounds [at Kingsmeadow in Trinity Without the Gates], finding ample time for satisfying lusts of appetite so that he near died of an excess of salmon caught at Passage on the estuary ... Twice Richard II, once Prince Hal came to Waterford ...

A crowded Shakespearean stage. I quote from Alan Downey's *The Glamour of Waterford* (1921). He may not have been overfond of our first English tourists. But he wrote the most delightful introduction to a city that has always seemed to me somewhat sphinx-like.

Leinster

◁ **St Mullins,** Carlow

High among the wonders and beauties of the River Barrow is the walk on the old towpath from Graignamanagh, and the restored abbey of Duisce in County Kilkenny, to St Mullins in Carlow, where tradition has it that St Moling founded a monastery in the seventh century. There is a small village, a most historic graveyard, a holy well, some monastic remains and, rising over all – to 1,694 feet – Brandon Hill.

There are more legends about St Moling than one can easily enumerate, but they are thoroughly dealt with in Maire MacNeill's *The Festival of Lughnasa.* Moling was a patron saint of Leinster, and the princely family of that province – the MacMurrough Kavanaghs – were patrons of the place. That family had long in its keeping the enshrined *Book of Mo-ling,* a seventh- or eighth-century gospel book written partly in Moling's own hand. It is now in the library of Trinity College, Dublin.

Nor do the legends of the place end with Moling and his fellow saints or with the mythological Gobaun-Saor, master craftsman of pagan Ireland. They come quite close to us and include the comic tale of Morgan Prussia Kavanagh, reputed in his day to be the tallest man in Europe, who lies buried in the graveyard.

▽ The Four Courts, Dublin

The River Liffey, James Joyce's Anna Livia Plurabelle, is a slender lady slipping through Dublin in slow, sinuous curves and wearing her graceful eighteenth-century bridges like bracelets. Here she encounters the baroque masses of one of Dublin's two great riverside classical buildings, James Gandon's Four Courts. Further downstream she receives a salute from his corresponding triumph of palladian purity, the Custom House. The Four Court's dome is echoed across the river by the solid Franciscan dome of Adam and Eve's church, named after the tavern in which it was located during days of religious persecution. Taking up the same domed theme is the tall tower and cupola of St Paul's, Arran Quay, an accomplished Neo-Grecian church by a Dublin master mason, Patrick Byrne.

Dublin and the Liffey, Dublin ▷

Dublin, the metropolis of Ireland, is situated in the province of Leinster, in the county of Dublin; at the bottom of a fine Bay, about eight miles in diameter; called after the city, Dublin Bay. The river Liffey, divides the town into nearly two equal parts, and empties itself into the bay about half a mile below the present city. Dublin is the second city in his Brittanic Majesty's dominions, and may rank with the very finest cities of Europe for extent, magnificence and commerce.

... Public structures of late years raised in Dublin, as the Parliament-houses, the Custom-house, Exchange, Law Courts, &c. are superb Edifices ...

(Malton's Dublin, 1799)

The Parliament House, now the Bank of Ireland, and probably the finest building in Dublin, can be seen at the top of Dame Street, the long, wide street running parallel and to the right of the Liffey. It faces the west front of Trinity College, whose four quadrangles are bounded on the far side by the green expanse of College Park. Opposite, on the north bank of the river, is the domed and porticoed Custom House, built by James Gandon in 1781. City Hall, a square temple of a building with giant Corinthian columns and a green dome, stands near the river on the south bank, almost facing Gandon's law courts, whose larger dome crowns an immense rotunda. The stone facing of the Four Courts is battle-scarred from bombardment by Free State troops during the Civil War.

To the south of City Hall is Dublin Castle, a replica of the 1790 original, which was burnt down in 1941.

Of the twentieth century, there are the city council silos, to the east of the castle; Liberty Hall, the trades union headquarters – a Dublin 'skyscraper' – looming over the Custom House; and near the mouth of the river, a new bridge, the first for decades. Where the 'river Liffey ... empties itself into the Bay' is Ringsend Power Station.

Frank McDonald of *The Irish Times* is one of the most intelligent and pugnacious defenders of Old Dublin against those who, desirous of wider vistas and more rapid transit, wish to widen the streets and flatten the past. He has strongly argued the case of those, including Dean Griffin of St Patrick's Cathedral, who feel that the widening of Patrick Street, to our left, and the consequent weight of traffic may affect the foundations of the cathedral, in the foreground. Jonathan Swift, the most famous Dean of all, sailed into his rest here.

To walk in the Cathedral's dim, devotional light is to give much thought to the twisted religious history of this country, pre- and post-Reformation. The little park is a pleasant place. Beyond is the cathedral close and Archbishop's Marsh's library, treasure house of antique books.

This picture, which could become historic, gives us a great deal of the heart of Old Dublin. Look beyond the red block of the comparatively modern Iveagh (Guinness) buildings to the other ancient cathedral, Christchurch, now alas, dominated by the white silos built to house city council officials. From the land or from the air those two structures cannot but strike the beholder with wonder. They were designed, we are told, to house officials of the city council, and the story of their erection on that historic site, and of the battle to preserve the Norse relics in Wood Quay, is now well known.

To the left is the dome of the Franciscan church on Merchants' Quay and the Catholic church of St Audeon and, hidden behind it, Old Audeon's, which is old enough to have a leper-squint.

Hidden there also is the last fragment of the old city walls, and Audeon's Arch; and, if antiquity gives you a thirst, there is the Brazen Head, the oldest pub, perhaps, in Ireland.

⊲ **Trinity College,** Dublin

The west front of Trinity College, the impressive group of eighteenth-century buildings that make up Dublin University, faces up Dame Street, its entrance flanked by the statues of Oliver Goldsmith and Edmund Burke. Facing them, where Dame Street melts into College Green, stands the declaiming figure of Henry Grattan, greatest of all Irish orators, who made some of his finest speeches in the Parliament House to his left, now a part of the Bank of Ireland – the most handsome part, combining Palladianism with baroque.

Behind the façade of the College are the twin wings of the chapel and the exam hall, their classical porticoes confronting each other across the stone quadrangle. On the left, set back from the chapel, is the dining hall, its roof sadly damaged by fire in 1984; on the right the splendid twenty-seven bay library, which houses the Book of Kells, a page of which is turned every day.

Beyond is College Park, where the ghost of Oliver St John Gogarty, wit, poet and athlete, rides round forever on a racing bike, and beyond that again is Pearse Street, called after Patrick Pearse, who was executed, with others, after the uprising of 1916.

◁ **Merrion Square and St Stephen's Green,**
Dublin

△ **Lambay Island,** Dublin

The book to take with you if you need a book, as you fly over Dublin, is Maurice Craig's classic, *Dublin, 1660–1860*, or *The Shell Guide to Ireland*, which does a thorough and exact job on the city.

Here are two of the great Dublin squares, both now open to the public, one recently, one for a long time. Closest to us is Merrion Square, laid out in 1762 by John Ensor for the Fitzwilliam Estate and about forty years in the building. So many notable people lived in it in the nineteenth century that to walk around it and study the plaques is to do a course in Irish history.

A little beyond the square are Leinster Lawn and Leinster House, once the town house of the Earl of Kildare and now inhabited by politicians. To compensate there is, close by, the Zoological Museum and the National Art Gallery, the College of Science, Government Buildings and, beyond Leinster House, the National Library and the National (Historical) Museum.

In the background is the largest of the squares, St Stephen's Green whose history as a public park, when it ceased to be a common with a resident gallows, goes back to the seventeenth century. The centre of Dublin – or of Ireland – is there. The Green, though, was never famous for its buildings and in recent years, it has both suffered and benefited from what we call development.

In the shadowy centuries Lambay was much afflicted by sea-rovers who used it as a jumping-off ground for mainland forays. So that little or no trace remains of its Columban monastic foundation. The island, now a bird sanctuary, is the property of Lord Revelstoke, of the Baring Brothers banking family; for his forebears Sir Edwin Lutyens, architect of some of the great monuments of Imperial India, grandly refurbished the castle and grounds. It is to Lord Revelstoke's steward that bird-watchers should apply for landing permission. Seals and sheep are also to be seen.

The last time the island was crowded was with prisoners at the end of the Williamite-Jacobite wars.

▽ **Blessington Reservoir,** Wicklow

When, fifty or so years ago, it was decided to dam the River Liffey at Poulaphuca, and flood the lovely and lonely Wicklow valley where the King's River joins the Liffey, there were quite natural protests. One English lover of Wicklow wrote that industrialization was writing Ireland's epitaph. That good man may have been over-reacting, and, as it happened, even if the beauty of the valley vanished under the waters, another beauty appeared in its place and added a new dimension to the already handsome village of Blessington.

The wandering lakes do their best for the fishermen and, seen from the hills, from the village of Lackan, or the old stone quarries of Ballyknockan (where there is a granite madonna, the primitive work of an old-time stone cutter), they give a perfect finish to the landscape.

Perhaps in the end the only loser was that shape-changing sprite or demon, the Pooka – second cousin to a modest English fellow by the name of Puck of Pook's Hill – for Poulaphuca, the Pooka's Pool, a deep gorge through which the river used to roar in flood, is now quiet. The turbines have sapped its strength.

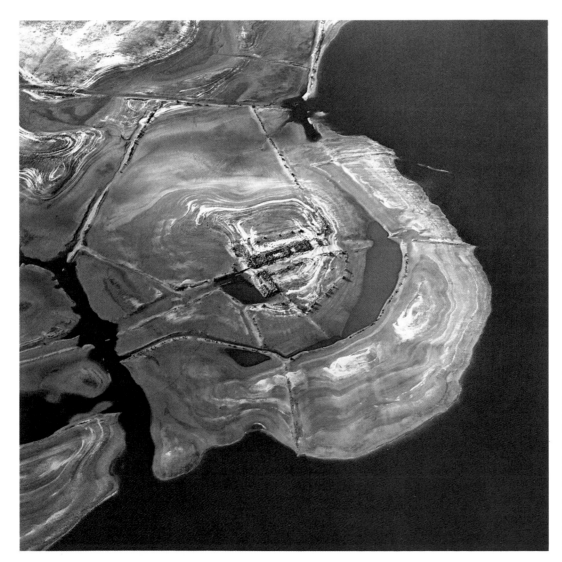

Dun Laoghaire, Dublin ▷

If you come to Ireland from the east and by sea, as an odd variety of people have done over the centuries, it is most likely that these will be the first welcoming arms that embrace you. For this is the harbour of Dun Laoghaire, or the fort of Laoghaire, high king of Ireland, we are told, round about the time in the fifth century when St Patrick arrived here. St Patrick also came from the east and by sea but not, the first time, of his own free will. But he grew to like the place and the people and, following a vision, came a second time and had some effect on our later development.

For one hundred and nine years of its existence, up to the change of government in the 1920s, Dun Laoghaire was called Kingstown, after another king. George IV sailed out from this harbour after his state visit to Dublin. Lord Byron celebrated the event:

But he comes! The Messiah of Royalty comes!
Like a goodly Leviathan roll'd from the waves;
Then receive him, as best such an advent he
   comes,
With a legion of cooks and an army of slaves!

As the speckled waters indicate, the harbour and the expanse of Dublin Bay outside the walls are the centre of yachting in Ireland; and Irish Lights, the lighthouse and lightship service, has its headquarters here. Although Dun Laoghaire is part of Greater Dublin it does very much preserve a separate – and equal identity. The East Pier to the left is a popular and crowded promenade, and the West Pier a place for meditative fishermen and whispering lovers. The town and its surroundings have been best written about by Padraic Colum in *The Flying Swans* and by L.A.G.Strong who, as a boy, spent holidays here.

◁ **Killiney,** Dublin

A young Dublin poet once complained that some people said: 'See Naples and die'. But he preferred to see Killiney and live. Which poet he was I cannot remember out of the standing army of one thousand poets that Patrick Kavanagh said were to be found in the pubs of our distinguished capital city. But he did make a certain point. Dalkey village, and Killiney Hill above it, were, when one was discovering Dublin, places of genuine wonder. There is still a charm in the old narrow streets and roadways ascending to the Victorianism of the park on Killiney Hill; and an exultation in looking south over the long strand and the lovely vale of Shanganah towards Bray Head and the mountains, and directly down on Dun Laoghaire harbour and Dalkey Island with its Queen and its protected (we hope) goats, and north across Dublin Bay to Howth Head. And on a clear day, and if your sight is good enough, you might envision the Carlingford Hills and send your eyes across the Border to Slieve Donard and the high Mournes. Ireland's too small to afford a border.

Dalkey has some slight Shavian associations because the great playwright's people had a summer nook there. Since then, though, both Dalkey and Killiney have been favoured with the presence of several literary men. Others get bogged down in Donnybrook.

◁ **Sandycove and Bulloch Harbour,** Dublin

On the tip of the promontory and on the top of the Martello tower, now a Joycean museum, stately, plump Buck Mulligan of Joyce's *Ulysses* forever comes, 'from the stairhead, bearing a bowl of lather on which a mirror and a razor [lie] crossed.' Down below the tower is the Forty-Foot swimming-pool reserved for 'Forty-Foot Gentlemen Only'. Recently there have been feminist incursions.

All sexes may safely sail into Bulloch Harbour.

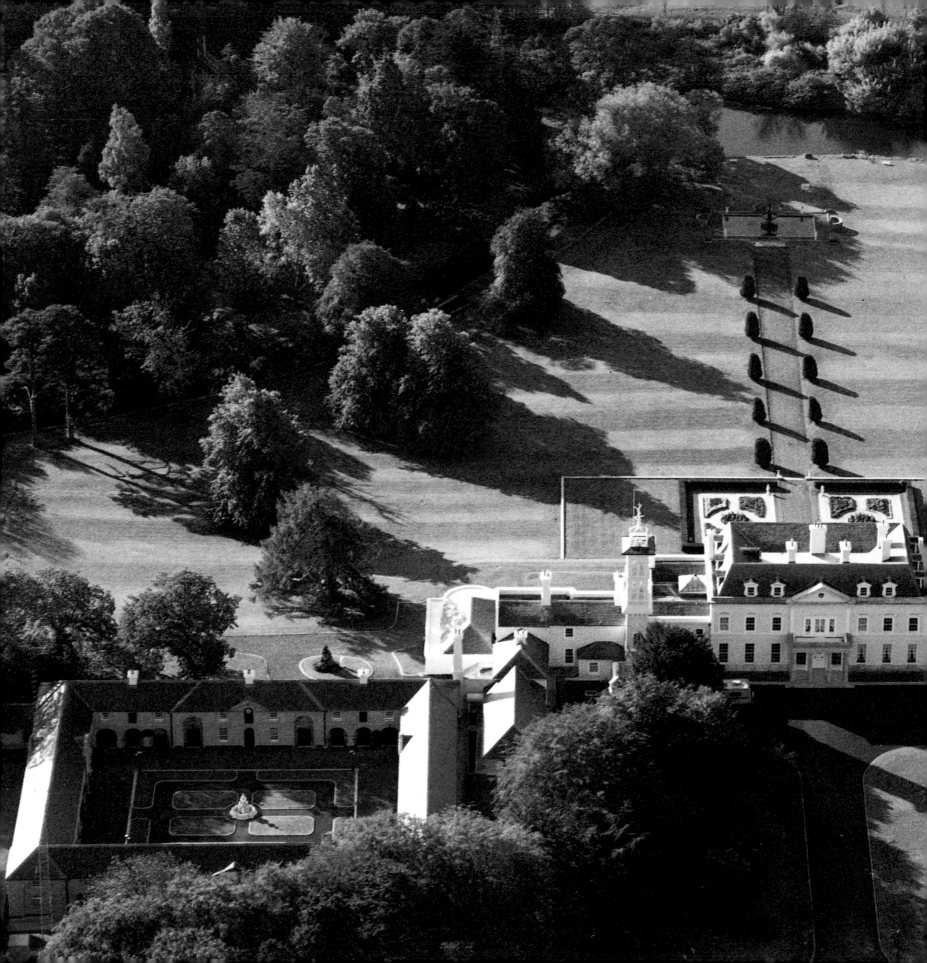

Straffan Lodge, Kildare

The Liffey goes quietly past under the trees in the background, and the bridge close to Straffan Lodge (or Lodge Park, Straffan) is a good spot from which to study Anna Livia Plurabelle (of Joyce's *Ulysses*) at about the middle state of her development. The house dates from 1795 and stands well on a rich riverine countryside notable for fine houses and much history.

A famous movie director lived here in recent years and was succeeded by an Iranian gentleman who could not, alas, return to the peace of the Liffeyside.

89

▽ St Patrick's College, Maynooth, Kildare

Oh hallowed cloisters of Maynooth! Oh happy walks! There at the feet of wise and holy men we learned lessons and were filled with noble thoughts to which were we but true, how happy were our lot ...

Far-flung across the world are the companions of our youth. Some sleep in holy Ireland ... Others lie beneath the pall of northern snows, and others rest to the dirge of the long wash of Australasian Seas ... in every strand our feet have been set, in every land we have made our home.

That was spoken in 1909 by Fr Peter Yorke, addressing the Maynooth Union in the great seminary in the County Kildare, and is quoted in Dr Jeremiah Newman's *Maynooth and Victorian Ireland* (Kenneys of Galway, 1983). Dr Newman continues:

[That] was fervid and it was florid, but it was true. By the end of the [nineteenth] century about a fifth of the Empire was Catholic; it contained nearly 170 Catholic bishops as against 90 Anglican. An impressive new basilica had been completed outside Madras. Truly, Maynooth had left its mark.

In January 1901, Queen Victoria died. For some years she had been unpopular with her own people. In Ireland she had become irrelevant. Yet she could not be said to have been anything other than a benefactor to Maynooth.

There may be other opinions on Maynooth. Yet even the most fervent anti-clerical could not question the importance of the College. And now that the gates are open to lay-students, it, and the neighbouring village, add up to an interesting part of the National University of Ireland.

Allenwood, Kildare ▷

A powerhouse is a powerhouse is a powerhouse, but the one we look at actually stands on the raw material from which the power comes – one of the vast peatbogs of the midlands.

Jane Barlow, a fiction-writer at the beginning of this century, sentimental and gentle, yet acute and observant and compassionate, loved the Irish bogland and described it as no other writer has done:

The broad level spreads away and away to the horizon, before and behind, and on either hand of you, very sombrely hued ... Heath, rushes, furze, ling, and the like have woven it thickly, their various tints merging, for the most part, into one uniform brown, with a few rusty streaks in it, as if the weather-beaten fell of some primeval beast were stretched smoothly over the flat plain. Here and there, however, the monochrome will be broken: a white gleam comes from a tract where the breeze is deftly unfurling the silky bog-cotton tufts on a thousand elfin distaffs ...

She had, though, being the daughter of a scholarly vice-provost of Trinity College, Dublin, a practical turn of mind and would have appreciated the modern application of milled peat to electric power.

◁ Castletown House, Celbridge, Kildare

The splendid Castletown, near Celbridge, adorns that portion of the Liffey valley and is a masterpiece of the early Georgian – serene and beautiful. It was built in 1722 for Speaker Connolly of the Irish House of Commons, who had risen from modest beginnings to being the richest man in the Ireland of his day. Both Edward Lovett Pearce, architect of the Dublin parliament house, and the Italian Alessandro Galilei provided plans. It was reputed to be the largest private house in Ireland, a detail that must have fascinated the domestic staff, or slave-labour, of the period. In our days, as the headquarters of the Irish Georgian Society, the mansion has been the inspirational centre of the effort to restore and preserve Georgian architecture. Close by are Leixlip and Maynooth and, as mentioned, Celbridge, with its Swift and Esther associations.

Connolly's Folly, Kildare ▷

This Conolly was no fool, but the eminent speaker of the Irish House of Commons in the eighteenth century. As was the fashion of the time, and for a long time after, this classical extravaganza closed a view, and ornamented the grounds of his great house of Castletown, near Celbridge, in the valley of the River Liffey. It was erected by Connolly's widow in 1740, probably to a design by William Castle.

'And straight will I repair', the girl sang in the old lovesong, 'to the Curragh of Kildare, and there find tidings of my dear.'

Her dear, in those days, had joined the British Army. Today it would be the Irish Army. The other reasons for repairing to the Curragh would be to farm sheep or, as the world knows that knows anything, to follow the horses.

Cloud shadows drift across the great plain. Fionn MacCumhaill sits forever on the Hill of Allen, or on what quarrying has left of the Hill of Allen. In Donnelly's Hollow, Donnelly, the long-armed bare-knuckle boxer, forever and for the honour of Erin flattened the Englishman, Cooper, Donnelly's right arm, or what's left of it, is in a glass case in a pub in Kilcullen.

Jack B. Yeats, using his paints lavishly, and his imagination of history, painted a picture of the famous bout.

△ **Athy,** Kildare

As I was a-walking the road to Athy
I saw an old petticoat hanging to dry . . .

It's a fine, rousing drinking-song and there's more to it, and a town as strong and dignified as Norman Athy, in the County of Kildare, can afford to laugh with and at such comparatively modern jingles. Here, on the upper reaches of the great River Barrow, Athy has been an important place for about seven hundred years.

The Earls of Kildare, the Geraldines, gave it their attention, and the castle, to defend the river-crossing, was built by the eighth Earl in 1506. Restored and preserved, it is still there under the name of White's Castle after a William White who rebuilt it in 1575. It can be seen here on the far bank of the River Barrow, to the left of the road bridge. Nearer the foreground of the picture is the Grand Canal, which joins the river just outside the town.

The name of the place remembers a Munster chieftain slain there in ancient battle, Ath-I, or the Ford of Ae, the unfortunate man in question, and not to be confused with the poet George Russell.

◁ Castlecomer, Kilkenny

The river, the Dinin Rua, looks harmless enough from the air. But it is one of those small streams that, when heavy rains fall, flood with a fury and rapidity that can be quite startling. It rushes down to join the noble Nore and it helps it onwards through Kilkenny city.

When you say Castlecomer to most people they think of coal and of the anthracite seam along the Leinster Ridge. But there is more to the town than that. Even from what we see of it, just from here, it is a mighty attractive small town, bright and airy, with none of the dust and sadness that we normally associate with the mining of coal – probably because the industry never did grow to any great proportions.

In the first half of the seventeenth century the land here fell into the hands of an Englishman, Sir Christopher Wandesford, who brought his own working people with him from across the water, including, of course, the miners.

Like most towns in Ireland, or anywhere else, Comer has seen its share of war. Only the high Himalayas and the Greenland Cap are exempt, and they may yet have their chance. It was last in the news in that way in 1798, when some of the Wexford rebels, falling back, made some sort of stand. There is a legend that when the rebels rushed for their powder they found that it had been wetted by natural means, by the Comer miners who were not Irish anyway. Serious historians are silent on the matter. But any reference to it, in pubs or public gatherings, can still, I have heard, give rise to some ill-feeling. The long memory!

Kilkenny Town, Kilkenny △

Historically, Kilkenny is, perhaps, the most interesting city in Ireland. That sounds like an extravagant statement when weighed against the claims of Dublin, Belfast, Derry, Galway, Limerick and Cork. Yet it is justified simply because here below us so much is contained in a small space and can be surveyed and understood as a compact unity. The Nore, one of the handsomest of Irish rivers, provides the centre for our picture even if the city, as do so many Irish settlements, turns its back on the water. From the air, as on the ground, the great Butler castle lords it over the river and the houses.

Here the past crowds so thickly around you that you might well be shouldered off the sidewalk by ghosts. There were, to begin with, the Butlers, those great Anglo-Norman Earls of Ormond, and all the history and conflict that their very presence in the place brought sweeping around those towers. Perhaps the most intense moment was in the 1640s when the city was the headquarters of the Catholic Confederation (the Confederation of Kilkenny), and the castle opened its gates in 1645 to Rinnucini, the papal nuncio. Oliver Cromwell, that restless tourist, was along later.

Many parliaments met here in earlier times, and in 1366 the Statutes of Kilkenny were enacted here in an effort to prevent the Anglo-Normans from becoming more Irish than the Irish themselves. What that meant was that they were to be mindful of their English King.

Where the Revenue Commissioners now crouch and conspire was once the Kilkenny Private Theatre.

On another level, but still in the world of the imagination, Kilkenny gave us, in 1324, one of Ireland's few witch-burning cases. The performers were Normans. Dame Alice Kyteler was charged with witchcraft, heresy and 'murderous assaults on her four husbands'. She fled to England and high influence saved her bacon. The lady was not for burning. Her servant, Petronilla, was burned in her stead. Hazards of domestic service. The Kyteler house may still be inspected. The ecclesiastical history of the place, from St Canice onwards, is rich: two great cathedrals, two great schools with lists of past pupils as long as the Nore.

▽ Jerpoint Abbey, Kilkenny

So many of the great monastic monuments of the past are, because of the attrition of troubled centuries, only picturesque ruins, but still capable of inspiring meditation. Jerpoint Abbey, close to Thomastown in the Nore valley in County Kilkenny, was one of the great Cistercian foundations. It was established originally by a king of Ossory, Donnchadh Mac Giolla Phádraig (Gillapatrick), a name and a gentility that survived into our own time in the person of Lord Castletown, a most cultivated man and friend of Douglas Hyde, scholar, poet, and president of the Irish Republic.

Monks came to Jerpoint from the monastery of Baltinglass, County Wicklow, in 1180. In its turn, Jerpoint sent out monks to other foundations.

When the visitors from over the water decided to keep the monasteries absolutely English, Jerpoint and Baltinglass were placed under the authority of Fountains Abbey in Yorkshire. It is ironically interesting to look down on it now and to reflect that in 1387 the abbot was fined for breaking one of the restrictive Statutes of Kilkenny and allowing Irishmen to become monks. For a ticket to heaven no Irish need apply.

At the Dissolution of the Monasteries, the abbey and its lands were leased by the English crown to the Earl of Ormond.

Now, all strife forgotten, it slumbers on rich, green land and you are free to hear, over the centuries the holy chant – and ignore the rest of it.

The Rock of Dunamase, Laois ▷

The storied and, over the centuries, much embattled rock stands up with notable distinction to the left of the road as you go from Monasterevan in County Kildare to Portlaoise, once called Maryborough, in County Laois, just as you cross the scraggy piece of open ground still called Maryborough Heath.

This midland county was and, to some extent, still may be the historic territory of the great clan of the O'Mores, and the rock was an effective fortress. The Normans found it so when they got here in the twelfth century. It was part of the dowry that went to the invader, Strongbow, with Aoife, daughter of Diarmuid MacMurrough, King of Leinster who, 'brought the Normans o'er', and who has been execrated ever since but who may have had his point of view.

The Normans, in a way that they had, made it a better fortress than it had been before. The O'Mores took it from the English in the fifteenth century and held it until those lands were planted under Mary Tudor. Hence Maryborough. But in the seventeenth-century wars of the Confederation of Kilkenny and of Cromwell it was again at the centre of the storm. One of the Cootes took it for Parliament. Then Owen Roe O'Neill, nephew of the great Hugh of Tyrone (and known as Don Eugenio for his years in the Earl of Tyrone's regiment in the Spanish service) took it back from the Confederation. The end of its wars came in 1650 when the Cromwellians stormed it and made sure it would never again be used as a fortress.

On a good day in summer it is a heavenly eminence on which to drowse and look down on the heart of Ireland. Not a sound to be heard but cattle calling and the whinnying wings of a snipe.

Abbeyshrule, Longford ▽

The river is the Inny, dreadfully regimented by drainage, as it flows from Lough Sheelin in the County Cavan, by way of Loughs Derryvara and Iron, to join the Shannon close to the town of Ballymahon. It is the 'shining river' of the poet John Keegan Casey, a harmless sort of rebel of the mid-eighteenth century who under the pen-name, Leo, wrote for the paper *The Nation*, organ of the Young Irelanders of 1848.

The pity is that the atrocities of our time have polluted even the old songs.

> Down beside the shining river the dark mass of
>   men was seen,
> High above the shining weapons hung their
>   own beloved green.
> Death to every foe and traitor. Forward, strike
>   the marching tune.
> And, hurrah, my boys, for freedom, 'tis the
>   Rising of the Moon'.

◁ Emo Court, Laois

Not more than a few miles away from the Rock of Dunamase and close to the town of Portarlington, where a boy who was to become the Duke of Wellington went for a while to school, is the stately house of Emo Court. The architect was James Gandon whose masterpieces, the Custom House and the Four Courts, still dignify Dublin city. Emo Court was built to his designs for the Earl of Portarlington in the last decade of the eighteenth century.

King Edward VII visited the house in the days of the Earl's occupation. A little above and to the right of centre can be seen a parallel parade of Wellingtonias that once marked the course of the demesne's main avenue. They move now into and are absorbed by State forestry. For the Royal visit that entire avenue, a mile long, was laid with red carpet. In 1938, in a hospital in the neighbouring town of Mountmellick, I talked with an old man who had been an army bugler as Edward passed by.

After the passing of the Portarlingtons the house was inhabited by the Jesuits, who employed it as a novitiate and a sort of home base for peripatetic missionary fathers. One of those years I spent there myself – as a novice, I hasten to add, who took his hand from the plough. In recent years it was purchased by Mr Cholmondley Harrison who has restored it to its lordly grandeur.

△ **Clogherhead,** Louth

On a map of the eastern coast, Clogherhead is a very slight protuberance a short distance north of the estuary of the Boyne River and the tragically historic town of Drogheda. Seen from the air, or the land if you go on foot from the village in the distance to the harbour in the foreground, it's an idyllic place, a sort of toy with the small harbour and pleasant landscape, and a beach for the admiration of the stray visitor and a few holidaymakers.

It has some historic associations with the seventeenth-century murdered or martyred Oliver Plunket, now honoured as a saint. In 1670, as Roman Catholic Archbishop of Armagh, he wrote, 'I am obliged to conceal myself by assuming the name of Captain Brown, wearing a sword and wig and carrying pistols.' After two quite scandalous trials for treason, one in Dundalk, one in London, he was hung, drawn and quartered at Tyburn on 11 July, 1681.

Carlingford, Louth

Beyond the narrow water the Mountains of Mourne sweep down to the sea, as they do in the celebrated song by Percy French.

Carlingford itself is a little paradise for the historian and antiquarian. One of its ancient Irish names was Cairlinn, and with the suffix it came to mean the fiord of Cairlinn. It rejoiced, also, in the names of Snamh-Ech, or the Swimming-Place of the Horses, and Snamh-Aighnech, after the Vikings who may also have washed in those waters. In AD 926 it is reported that an Irish king, splendidly named Muirchertach of the Skin Cloaks, there cut the heads off two hundred Viking sea-rovers. But we must remember that the Department of Statistics was not, at that time, up to its contemporary exactitude.

The Normans came in the twelfth century under the notable Hugh de Lacy. King John slept here for three nights. The atmosphere and appearance of that long street, with several notable ancient buildings, bring the meditative mind back easily into the past. It is a curio of a town.

The Boyne, Louth

Even the weariest river, as we are informed on very good authority, winds somewhere safe to sea; and where the Boyne comes to the Irish Sea between the villages of Mornington and Baltray it has indeed the appearance of a river weary with a weight of history and mythology.

It starts off in life uncertainly, with some faint intention of going west but changing its mind rapidly and going determinedly eastwards, taking with it through quiet green country a long story and mingled traditions.

It passes close to Clonard, where there was a famous ancient monastery. It leaves, a few miles to the right, Summerhill, where the Duke of Wellington spent some of his boyhood. It flows through the town of Trim, with its tremendous Norman fortress known as King John's Castle, and its Yellow Steeple which isn't really a steeple but by which, a local tradition holds, the Cromwellians sighted their guns. It flows under Bective Bridge and by the ancient ruin of Bective Abbey. Across the river at Bective is Dunsany Castle.

The river passes by the Hill of Tara, to be joined at the town of Navan by the Leinster Blackwater. About the valleys of the two rivers Sir William Wilde, father of Oscar, wrote that classical book *Beauties of the Boyne and Blackwater*. From Navan to the estuary of the Boyne, take that book with you and encounter everybody from St Patrick to King William to Cromwell (again!) and to King Cormac MacAirt, one of the first Irishmen, or so it is said, to hearken to the Christian message.

All of this is not discernible from the air but might be from eternity or outer space.

◁ **Dundalk,** Louth

Emerging from those shadowy places in which poets and patriots found inspiration and images, Dundalk has had an exciting history right from 1186, when it came into existence under the Normans. When the English, or whatever you wish to call them at that time, decided seriously to move into Ireland, this was one of their strong points and a jumping-off ground for attacks on the O'Neills and O'Donnells and other clans of Ulster.

Three times it was burned by O'Neills, once by an O'Donnell, once by Edward Bruce who was crowned King of Ireland in the neighbourhood in 1316 in a curious dream of Pan-Celtic monarchy. The waves of the wars of the sixteenth and seventeenth centuries swept around it.

The river, of which we see the estuary, comes down from the hills of South Armagh, from around Forkhill and Crossmaglen, and beyond the water are the Carlingford hills and the Cooley peninsula.

Monasterboice, Louth ▷

The valley of the River Boyne eastward, say, from Bective Bridge and the Hill of Tara and the Hill of Slane to the sea, may well have been, in history and prehistory, the most crowded corner of Ireland. Green mounds mark the sites of the palaces of ancient kings. How palatial those palaces may or may not have been is a matter for poets.

A rickety bridge at a river crossing marks the spot where James II and William of Orange contended for the crown of England; and a few miles away and slumbrous in the peace that surrounded 'holy men who had a hand in heaven' are the crowded ancient stones of Monasterboice, the monastery of St Buithe or Boyne. There are many forms of the name, but nobody knows anything about the man except that he is said to have died in the early sixth century.

The famous round tower, though no longer complete, still soars one hundred feet above the other relics of monastic settlement: flat gravestones, two churches, a sundial that noted the days passing into centuries, high crosses on which you may have read scriptural stories carved into figures – David killing the lion and the bear, Abraham and Isaac, the children in the fiery furnace, etc.

Flann of Monasterboice is the most notable name out of the saintly centuries. But there is a tradition that, much later, Saint Oliver Cromwell passed below there and that he, or some of his disciples, did damage to the North Cross. But where in Ireland by tradition was he not? Certainly he was downstream at Drogheda, where he damaged more than crosses.

▽ **Trim**, Meath

By road you come into the town of Trim at the bottom right-hand corner of our picture. You have just passed the ruins of the ancient abbey with their quite astounding echo. The river is the Boyne.

There are, you might say, two towns in Trim: the busy market-town of the present and another town of ancient and most impressive ruins – and of ghosts, Norman and Irish and Elizabethan and Cromwellian, and more, that go with them. The great De Lacy Castle, King John's castle, is one of the best examples in the country of how medieval men endeavoured to keep strangers from intruding on their domesticity. There are fragments of an ancient town wall, and a column in honour of Wellington who lived here for a while when he was young.

The tall tower in the background is known as the Yellow Steeple, although it doesn't look like a steeple of any colour and was, in fact, a bell tower built in the fourteenth century over the Augustinian monastery of St Mary. There is a tradition that the Cromwellians used it to sight their guns.

Follow that semi-circle of street and swing left for Athboy and Delvin, and the Vale of Fore and other quiet corners of Meath and Westmeath. But if you are interested in the past, and if you like to linger in a pleasant town, you may stay a long time in Trim.

◁ **Drogheda**, Louth

It was once the custom for loyal Orangemen to stand up in the railway carriage when the train crossed the River Boyne on that stately viaduct. That was to honour the glorious, pious and immortal memory of King William who had also crossed the river, upstream, there at Oldbridge in the dim distance of our picture. Oliver Cromwell had passed this way about forty years before William, and in the September of 1649 stormed the town, making sure that he would be remembered by what he would have considered the exemplary slaughter of about two thousand of the garrison. The survivors had free transport to slavery in the Barbadoes.

The origins of the town, which is thirty miles north of Dublin, go back to the Norse sea-rovers, and to the English it was of a strategic importance that made it almost the rival of the city to the south. Parliaments met here, including the assembly that in 1494 enacted Poyning's Law, extending to Ireland 'all statutes concerning the public weal made within the realm of England'. Fragments of the old fortifications, notably the striking St Laurence's Gate, are still to be seen. In the Catholic church on the main street there is preserved the embalmed head of the martyred St Oliver Plunket, (1629–81) Archbishop of Armagh, to which shrine pilgrims come.

It is a handsome, bustling town and one of the gateways to the treasures, scenic and archaeological, of the Boyne valley.

At an agricultural show close to the town of Kells (on the horizon), and on the bountiful grasslands of Meath, a cub reporter from Dublin once asked a local veteran what was that there tower on the hill. He was told that it was a lighthouse and later he began his story by mentioning the attractive seaside town of Kells.

It is by no means a lighthouse although it looks like one and was meant to look like one, and Kells is about thirty miles from the sea; and the veteran was unkind.

The curious tower tops the Hill of Lloyd which rises to about four hundred feet over the distant sea and, since the tower stands at a hundred feet, it was clearly designed to provide a fine prospect over the flat land. But its principle purpose was to commemorate one Sir Thomas Taylor, and it was put there in 1791 by his son, also Thomas, and first Earl of Bective.

Kells is a mile and a bit away, and pressed down and flowing over with ancient history, and hoary with old stones and crosses and monastic memorials.

△ **Athcarne Castle,** Meath

The Elizabethan tower house at Athcarne, three miles from the village of Duleek in County Meath, was built by William de Bathe in 1587. It was later extended with a long wing and later still given an eighteenth-century stable block.

William de Bathe was a distinguished and accomplished son of the Norman gentry of the Pale, a student at Oxford University and a grand-nephew of the Earl of Kildare, to whom he dedicated a treatise called 'A Brief Introduction to the Art of Music'. He was a favourite of Queen Elizabeth and presented her with a new harp of his own devising.

After his death his widow, Janet, commemorated him in a series of wayside stone crosses which dot the countryside around. One, in the middle of the village green at Duleek, depicts a number of saints including the Irish saints St Ciaran and St Patrick. The finest example, the White Cross, is just across the river from the castle on the Duleek-Balrath Road. It has a crucifixion, a Virgin and Child and some good Renaissance detail.

◁ **Newgrange,** Meath

The restoration of the prehistoric burial mound of Newgrange has been one of the several impressive achievements of Irish archaeologists in recent years. The valley of the river Boyne here, between Slane and Drogheda, is rich beyond description in ancient remains; Knowth, Dowth, Newgrange, to mention the most important. Work is still proceeding on the neighbouring great cairn of Knowth.

Newgrange is about fifty feet in height and almost six times that in diameter. Through a narrow passage underground you can enter into the central chamber, and study the carven stones and meditate on the nothingness of one brief life.

It is common nowadays for decent people to establish contact with our shadowy forebears by visiting the great cairn at the time of equinox to study the behaviour of, and perhaps in their secret hearts to worship, the sun.

Hill of Tara, Meath ▷

If those hot-gospellers who once dug into the Hill of Tara in search of the Ark of the Covenant had ever seen it like this, as the Seraphim may see it, they would have felt perfectly justified: there must be something down there. Alas, there is little except the whispering and illimitable grasslands of Meath, and the assurance that we have been reared by legend to accept: that here was the ancient abode of the High Kings of Ireland. How high were the Kings?

Unquestionably Tara of the Kings was an important place in ancient religious belief, whatever that may have been, on this island. But with the coming of Christianity its importance departed. The Kings had already departed to other parts of Ireland, even to the far north-west. But by association they still called themselves Kings of Tara. Legends accumulated around this place, a slight grassy eminence in a wide grassland. A day spent in inspecting its ancient remains can be rewarding: Adamnan's cross, the Fort of the Synods, the Fort of the Kings, the Mound of the Hostages, Laoghaire's Fort, the Banqueting Hall and, perhaps, the loveliest place on the hill, Gráinne's Fort, which may or may not have something to do with that Gráinne who fled in the company of Diarmuid before the wrath of Fionn.

Bring a good guidebook and savour the legends. The gentle midland peace is helpful to such meditations. Modern excavation has revealed remarkable things, going back over four thousand years.

'Twas on a day when Kings did fight beside the
    Boyne's dark water,
And thunder roared from every height, and
    earth was red with slaughter,
That morn an aged chieftain stood apart from
    mustering bands,
And, from a height that crowned the flood
    surveyed broad Erin's lands.

There are many ballads about the event on the
Boyne, the last European battle (1690) fought on
Irish soil. The height that crowned the flood was to
the left of our picture. The aged chieftain was
Frederick Schomberg, or Schonberg, General for
William of Orange, who was famous on far foreign
fields, and who died there at the age of eighty-two.
He remained there, in monumental form, until he
was blown up by enthusiastic Irish patriots about
fifty, or perhaps more, years ago: one of the first of
our conquerors to leave Ireland by air.

The Williamites made two main river crossings,
one to the left, one further upstream. The Jacobites
fell back southward and the last shots of the battle,
tradition says, were fired out there on the horizon at
the defile of Duleek. On Duleek Common, and
almost within living memory, relics of the battle –
coins, bullets, bones – were unearthed.

The river is the Shannon spreading like a sea, as
Spenser noted. Or lazing its way through the flat
midlands. The powerhouse proves that Ireland is
with it – meaning the modern world. The village is
Shannonbridge, and the bridge is discernible. But
the most interesting object (not discernible) in the
neighbourhood is a nineteenth-century military
fort built on the west bank of the Shannon to keep
the Connachtmen out of the rest of Ireland, or,
perhaps, the rest of Ireland out of Connacht.
Nobody has ever worked it out.

▽ The Town of Birr, Offaly

Many quite startling events happened in the orderly and gracious town of Birr, County Offaly. On a certain day in Dooley's Hotel in the main square, a journalist, who was a friend of mine, picked up the buzzing telephone and found himself talking to a Queen who thought she was about to talk to a Princess who was holidaying in a castle in the neighbourhood. Until the day he died the journalist maintained that his presence was a complete accident. But he never did deny that it made good matter for London's Fleet Street.

On another day, the hard-riding country gentlemen of Galway managed, in a moment of festivity and quite by accident, to burn down that hotel and earn themselves the name of Galway Blazers. The activities of such courtly incendiaries can best be studied in the early novels of Charles Lever (1806–72).

But Birr sent them back to Galway and remained, as I have said, orderly and gracious, perhaps more so than any other town in Ireland. From this viewpoint it looks just like that.

◁ Birr Castle, Offaly

This was once the land of the O Carrolls of Éile until an invader, by the name of Parsons (the family later became Earls of Rosse), came in from Norfolk and laid the foundations of the town of Birr, which, for a long time, was known as Parsonstown.

It was the third Earl of Rosse (1800–67) who, from the grounds of Birr Castle, discovered the Spiral Nebulae with the Great Telescope which he had invented. He made himself and Birr, or Parsonstown, famous in the world of science.

His observatory can be seen between the trees in the middle of our picture. The Great Telescope is in the Science Museum in London.

The great castle was enlarged and modernized in the nineteenth century by Francis Johnston and other architects.

Like most towns anywhere, Birr changed hands and went up and down during the wars, but the Parsons family remained. As we may see when we take a look at the Castle, which was once better equipped to have a look at us.

▽ Clonmacnoise, Offaly

T. W. Rolleston (1847–1920) was, and by this is he most remembered, the poet who wrote the lines (after a fourteenth-century Irish poem) that sum up the past, living forever, of Clonmacnoise, perhaps the most famous of all our ancient monastic settlements, founded in the sixth century on the banks of the wide and slumbering Shannon some miles south of Athlone:

> In a quiet, watered land, a land of roses,
> Stands St Kieran's city fair
> And the warriors of Erin, in their famous
>   generations
> Slumber there.

> There beneath the dewy hillside sleep the
>   noblest
> Of the Clan of Conn,
> Each below his stone, his name in branching
>   Ogham
> And the sacred knot thereon.

> There they laid to rest the seven kings of Tara,
> There the sons of Cairbre sleep,
> Battle-banners of the Gael that in Kieran's plain
>   of crosses
> Now their final hosting keep.

> And in Clonmacnoise they laid the men of Teffia,
> And right many a lord of Breagh.

> Deep the sod above Clan Creide and Clan
>   Conaill,
> Kind in hall and fierce in fray.

> Many and many a son of Conn, the Hundred-
>   fighter,
> In the red earth lies at rest.
> Many a blue eye of Clan Colman the turf covers,
> Many a swanwhite breast.

Much of the extensive remains date from the great period of endowment in the twelfth century.

Lough Derryvaragh, Westmeath ▷

Three hundred years they flew over Lough Derryvaragh and swam on its waters. Often their father, King Lír, came to the lake and called the three swans to him and caressed them. Often their kinsfolk came to talk with them. Often harpers and musicians came to listen to the wonder of their singing. When three hundred years were ended the swans rose suddenly and flew far and far away . . .

That's a fragment from Ella Young's rendering of the sad tale of the Children of Lír, who by evil enchantment were changed into swans. Three hundred years they spent there on the waters of Derryvaragh, the most beautiful of the midland lakes. Three hundred years they spent on the cold and bitter sea of Moyle that flows between Ireland and Scotland, then three hundred more on the Western Sea.

Blessedly, they came for a while under the protection of a Christian saint, but were rudely restored to human shape by the touch of a King from the North:

> He came to the altar, and the swans were close to it. He put his hands on the swans to take them by force. When he touched them the swan-feathers dwindled and shrivelled and became as fine dust, and the bodies of Lir's children became as a handful of dust, but their spirits attained to freedom and joined their kinfolk in the Land-of-the-Ever-Living.

In the folklore of that Irish lakeland, and in many other parts of the world, the swan is a sacred bird.

In the Garden of Remembrance in Parnell Square in Dublin the legend is honoured in splendid statuary by the late Oisín Kelly.

◁ **Athlone**, Westmeath

If Ireland has a centre, or if the Irish do, it could, perhaps, be placed here, at the Ford of Luan, the crossing at Athlone of the great River Shannon: Westmeath and Leinster to the right of the picture, Roscommon and Connacht to the left, and in the background the hint of the wide expanses of Lough Ree, one of the greatest of the Shannon lakes.

The importance of the river crossing meant that the place accumulated more than its share of violent history, right from the days of the ancient kings to the thunderous culmination of the Williamite and Jacobite wars.

In July of 1690, a memorable month and a memorable year, ten thousand of William's soldiers attacked the town, which was valiantly defended by the Jacobite Irish under Colonel Richard Grace. But a year later along came the Dutch General Ginkel with twice as many Williamite men. The town, whose defenders numbered but fifteen hundred, fell to assault in the lead up to the Jacobite and Irish debacle of the Battle of Aughrim – which was also – almost – the end of Gaelic Ireland. The dreadful bombardment by 'the grim Dutch gunners', and the heroic exploits of Custume and a few others who broke down the bridge, have given us one of our most vivid patriotic legends, celebrated by Aubrey de Vere in a poem that begins with the not noticeably modest statement: 'Does any man dream that a Gael can fear?'

Today, all passion spent, Athlone, to the passer-by, seems just a prosperous and hospitable town – from which you may take boats provided by Coras Iompair Eireann (The Irish Transport Company) to explore the lordly Shannon, upstream as far as Lough Key, downstream by the noble remains of perhaps the greatest of the ancient monastic places, Clonmacnoise, and on to Lough Derg and Killaloe and the fringe of Limerick city.

Clonyn Castle, Delvin, Westmeath

This impressive building is, or was, the seat of the Nugents, Earls of Westmeath, who go back to Gilbert de Nangle (de Angulo), brother-in-law to that notable Norman Hugh de Lacy, who was much around in the twelfth century in these parts. De Lacy gave to Nangle the barony of Delvin, and the

Nangles or Nugents produced many notable people, including a Father Francis Nugent who, in his time, was described as one of the most learned men in Europe. In 1591 he joined the Capuchin friars, and introduced that order of priests into Ireland where it still flourishes.

One of the exciting stories of this locality concerns the village of Delvin and the minor civil war that took place there when in the 1920s Brinsley MacNamara wrote the novel *The Valley of the Squinting Windows*. The people of the place may have over-identified. Brinsley's friendship I was privileged to have and his memory I cherish, and I have travelled much with him, not in Concord but in Delvin. At Collinstown Cross nearby, a man told

me that when he was young it was a favourite thing to cycle into Delvin on a Saturday night to see the people fighting up and down the street about the book. Which was, also, burned on the village street, and an old lady said, 'Thank God, the trouble's over. The book's burned.'

An innocent age!

The other story concerns Lawrence of Arabia and the neighbouring big house and estate of the Chapmans, of whom he was, shall we say, a connection but with no claim on house or land. A local legend has it that he would come to Dublin, leap on his great motorbike, ride to Delvin and round the Chapman estate wall, and away again.

A strange ghost!

◁ **New Ross,** Wexford

New Ross steps up in terraces like a Rhineland town, from the wide River Barrow which has by now absorbed the Nore and is on the way to meet the Suir and be absorbed by the southern sea.

'The Boys of Wexford' by P. J. MacCall has it:

'We bravely fought and conquered at Ross and
  Wexford town,
Three Bullet Gate, for years to come, will speak
  of our renown . . .'

Fair enough, they bravely fought, even to the extent of one poor fellow putting his arm down the hole of a cannon and crying out that he 'had her shtopped'. But they did not conquer. For in the bloody misery, in 1798, of a people goaded by misgovernment into red rebellion, two thousand rebels died here on the steep slope above the river and the town was almost totally destroyed by fire. A portion of Three Bullet Gate is still to be seen.

The town (apart, that is, from the original monastic foundation of the sixth century) was founded by the Norman William the Marshall, Earl of Pembroke, and his wife, Isabella, heiress of Strongbow and Aoife, daughter of Dermot MacMurrough, King of Leinster. In the fourteenth century the ill-led forces of Richard II, and of Art MacMurrough, a more respected member of that princely family, fought around the place. Art held it for a long time and died here in 1418.

Cromwell, like Kilroy, was here. Cromwell was most everywhere. He crossed the big river on a bridge of boats and, the rumours of his mopping-up operations at Drogheda and Wexford having gone before him, the garrison prudently surrendered.

Fr Cullen, the Jesuit who founded the Pioneer Total Abstinence Association, was a New Ross man. There is a plaque to him on the wall of the Tholsel. It could not so well have gone on the wall of his birthplace which is now a public house.

Kilmore Quay, Wexford ▷

The baronies of Forth and Bargy make up a unique area, in customs and once even in language, in the extreme south of the County Wexford. Which terminates, most decidedly, in a point at Kilmore Quay. Beyond that there are only the Saltee Islands, inhabited by cats and goats and seabirds.

The thatched cottages of Kilmore Quay are worth travelling a long way to see. The parish church is famous for carols and the honour of singing them passes on from generation to generation.

△ **Wexford Town,** Wexford

Enniscorthy, Wexford ▷

More than a thousand years of history are down there, for as long ago as all that the Norse set up a trading post where the Slaney, coming all the way from Lugnaquillia and the Wicklow mountains, meets the extreme south-western sea. Further down the coast the Normans came in at the strand of Baginbun and, in 1169, Wexford was taken by Dermot MacMurrough, King of Leinster. It became the first Irish settlement to fall into Anglo-Norman hands. Five hundred years later Cromwell made it the stage for one of his more striking and most treacherous massacres. The fighting of 1798, and the variety in atrocity, left many ghosts here. In long, quiet periods and over the centuries Wexford prospered, a busy, industrious, friendly town.

The river is the Slaney, in the south-east of the country, and at this point, just as high up as the tidal water can reach. In 1798 the fighting of the ill-fated Wexford Rebellion swept around, and as good as ended in, the neighbourhood of this town of Enniscorthy. Eight miles away is Boolavogue or Boleyvogue and 'the bright May meadows of Shelmalier', where on a night in the May of that year Crown forces burned down some houses and the Catholic chapel, and the house of the parish priest, the renowned Fr John Murphy. It was the last spark to touch off the brooding violence with which the air was already overladen: Fr Murphy led the rebels and found his place in history and balladry and was brutally executed in the town of

Tullow in County Carlow.

The rebels took Enniscorthy, marched on to Wexford town, and in the inevitable final retreat and defeat came back to Vinegar Hill, beside this town, where they had set up their central camp in the brief moment of victory. Here they were overwhelmed by twenty thousand troops under Generals Lake and Johnson. General Lake was not notorious for the giving of quarter.

This is an interesting, handsome town in a very beautiful river valley. Three miles downstream Spenser meditated for a while on his Faerie Queene. A mile away, but a long time later, there was born at Borrowdale a boy who was to command the British Fleet in the First World War, Admiral the Earl Beatty.

▽ **J.F.K. Memorial Park,** Wexford

When John F. Kennedy was a young fellow he visited these parts where his people came from, near the town of New Ross down at the far end of County Wexford. He made friends then, whom he remembered and who remembered him on the day of the triumphal return visit of 1962: triumphal for the Irish here and there and for the man himself and his own people. As a journalist I was present on that day and can testify to the triumph and the happiness. He vowed to return in the Spring and, as we know, he did not. The best memorial to both triumph and tragedy is this simple mark on the ground of Ireland.

Sugarloaf Mountain, Wicklow ▷

We are looking west into the Wicklow mountains, over Bray Head which humps out over the large resort town of Bray at the southern boundary of Dublin Bay. The hill in the middle distance is the Little Sugarloaf, and beyond is the quartz cone, 1,659 feet high, of the Great Sugarloaf. There was an earlier, more poetic Irish name, supplanted by that dreadful anglicism. The coastal belt of Wicklow, like Killarney, suffered from being a popular sightseeing place in the nineteenth century. Beyond that belt is the Wicklow of John Millington Synge, as you will find it in his notebook, *In Wicklow and West Kerry*, and in the play *In the Shadow of the Glen*. But taken all in all, County Wicklow is very beautiful and Dubliners are particularly blessed in having such a paradise on the fringe of the city.

▽ Powerscourt, Wicklow

Close to Enniskerry is the great house of Powerscourt, originally built, in 1731–40, by Richard Cassels for the Wingfields, Viscounts Powerscourt. That family is no longer there. The great house was damaged some years ago by a calamitous fire, in which all the magnificent contents perished. But the splendid gardens, now the property of an American gentleman, are open to the public for a small fee; and there is also the waterfall, an impressive cataract, a Tennysonian downward smoke, and a favourite place for sightseers. When George IV came to Powerscourt in 1821 the waterfall was dammed up in order to give him an exciting spectacle: while the royal party watched from a specially constructed bridge the sluice gates were to be opened. However, the king spent too long over his dinner and never got to the waterfall – which was just as well, for when the water was later released the bridge was swept away.

In the days of Victorian tourism and for some time afterwards, Enniskerry was frequently referred to as Ireland's Swiss village. It is certainly hilly and handsome. Beyond that is Calary Lake and Calary Bog, from which the Liffey, Joyce's Anna Livia Plurabelle, emerges. And the dark beauty of the Wicklow Mountains. Synge country.

◁ Wicklow Town, Wicklow

About Wicklow town Lochlinn McGlynn wrote: 'This is the town where Ireland ends.'

He meant it in no uncomplimentary fashion. But merely that if you walk the tidy streets, or venture out towards the crown of Wicklow Head, you do get a sense of finality and completeness. Even if from far off Howth Head you look south and see, beyond Bray Head, that promontory of Wicklow you may get the notion that you are glimpsing Hy-Brazil or the farthest Hebrides.

Patrick and Palladius, it is said, both tried to come ashore here at different times but were refused admission by the local boss. His name may have been Byrne. About a thousand years later the Byrnes tried hard to dissuade less saintly foreigners from landing. The power of the great Wicklow sept of O'Byrne was broken by the beginning of the seventeenth century. Yet the foreigners no longer cut such a wide swathe in Wicklow, or anywhere else, and the O'Byrnes are still there.

Leamore Strand, Wicklow

On the horizon to the north are the Sugarloaves and Bray Head. The railway from Dublin to Wexford town parallels this long strand that from above looks as if it had been done with a plumbline and plaster and a careful trowel.

Sean O'Faolain in a strange story, 'Murder at Cobbler's Hulk', in a 1976 collection, *Foreign Affairs* (Constable), is not too happy about this stretch of coastline:

A single line, rarely used, continues the railway, beside this beach, on and on, so close to the sea that in bad winters the waves pound in across the track, sometimes blocking it for days on end with heaps of gravel, uprooted sleepers, warped rails. When this happens, the repair gangs have a dreary time of it. No shelter from the wind and spray. Nothing to be seen inland but reedy fields, an occasional farmhouse or abandoned manor, a few leafless trees decaying in the arid soil or fallen sideways. And, always, endless fleets of clouds sailing away towards the zinc-blue horizon.

It looks better in the picture: and westward, on a clear day, there is a heartening vision of the Wicklow mountains.

Connacht

Galway Bay, Galway

'Tis far away I am today from scenes I roamed a
  boy,
And long ago the hour, I know, I first saw
  Illinois.
But time nor tide nor waters wide can wean my
  heart away.
For, ever true, it flies to you, my dear old Galway
  Bay.
O grey and bleak, by shore and creek, the rugged
  rocks abound,
But sweet and green the grass between, as
  grows on Irish ground.
So friendship fond, all wealth beyond and love
  that lives always,
Bless each good home beside your foam, my
  own dear Galway Bay.

That was Francis A.Fahy (1854–1935) who wrote
most of the best songs about Galway and the land
around it.

He was a Kinvara man, from the south of the bay,
and spent most of his life as a civil servant in
London, and his spare time in promoting in the
great Babylon the cause of Irish Ireland. With
overpowering nostalgia, the best of his songs return
to the shores of this wide and windy water, as, for
instance, 'The Ould Plaid Shawl' and 'The Queen of
Connemara'.

One of the bay's famous oyster beds, the Red
Bank, is or was somewhere off Kinvara and gave its
name to a once noted Dublin city fish restaurant
which is now, oddly enough, a church.

But the bay's oysters have, in spite of that lapse,
become even more famous over the last twenty or
so years with the establishment and success of an
annual Lucullan oyster festival.

◁ The Aran Islands, Galway

The bleak and beautiful Aran Islands span the mouth of Galway Bay. In the foreground is Rock Island, with Brannock Island behind and, in the middle distance, the largest of these desolate outcrops, Inishmore. Beyond are Inishmaan and Inisheer, receding almost to the skyline and the cliffs of County Clare.

△ The Aran Islands, Galway

'I was born on a stormswept rock and hate the soft growth of sunbaked lands where there is no frost in mens' bones.' That was Liam O'Flaherty, great novelist and short-story writer and extraordinary man, and that is the stormswept rock on which he was born: Inishmore.

The impressive structure in the foreground and clinging to the cliff edge is Dún Aengus, generally acknowledged to be one of the finest prehistoric monuments in western Europe, and a mystery of the sea to the islanders and to everybody else. There was an earlier name that had nothing to do with Aengus, mythological chieftain of another of those mythological peoples, the Fir Bolg.

W.B. Yeats sent John Synge to the islands to express a way of life that had never been expressed. Synge might have gone without being sent, yet the influence of Yeats was all-important.

The islands remain remote and unique, but Liam O'Flaherty in 'The Black Soul', and in many of his best short stories, has expressed the way of life on his stormswept rock as no one else has done, or could do. Another O'Flaherty, Robert, not a native, made the film 'Man of Aran'.

◁ **Galway City,** Galway

Galway is, of all the cities and towns in Ireland, the one most possessed by water: living water, wild water, clean water, sea water, river water, lake water, but not water in the whiskey except you put it there yourself.

In the right foreground is Galway Harbour, a busier place normally than it seems to be at this moment. The boat takes off from there for the Aran Islands, unless you wish to fly, as nowadays you can. At the left of the rushing Galway River (the running of the salmon is one of the sights of the year), you may find what is left of the poor district known as the Claddach, and in the background are the wide and windy reaches of Loch Corrib.

W.B. Yeats boasted of an ancestor who traded out of Galway into Spain, and the Spanish connection in that city for a long time was strong and evident. F.R. Higgins, in his fine elegy on his friend, the Gaelic storyteller Padraic O Conaire, whose statue sits in Eyre Square in the centre of the city, wrote:

And women in the grassy streets of Galway
Will hearken for his passing, but in vain,
Will hardly hear his steps, as shadows lengthen
Through archways of forgotten Spain.

The reference may be a general one to old, narrow, winding streets or it may be particular, referring to the famous Spanish Arch down there by the edge of the water: and it may be said right away that the streets are not all that grassy. Eyre Square is, but Galway is a busy, industrious place. Yet we know what the poet means, and Galway still does preserve an air of antiquated, mercantile gentility and of a time in history when gentlemen thought of other things than making money. Like duelling, for instance, or hanging your own son for murder.

There is a theory that you always stay another day in Galway and, certainly, the cordiality and conviviality of the capital city of the Gaeltacht has been known to affect even the most regular and businesslike. Particularly when the annual Races come round at Ballybritt:

There was half a million people there of all
  denominations,
The Catholic, the Protestant, the Jew, the
  Presbyterian.
There was yet no animosity, no matter what
  persuasion,
But fáilte and hospitality inducing fresh
  acquaintance.

For the quincentenary of the City of the Fourteen Tribes, Kennys of Galway reproduced, among other relevant publications, James Hardiman's *History of Galway*, first published in 1820. It is a colourful and resonant story.

Kilconnell Friary, Galway

On the road from Galway city to the town of Ballinasloe this striking monastic ruin may give pause even to the most casual horseman passing by. It was a Franciscan friary, dating from the middle of the fourteenth century and founded by and under the patronage of the O'Kelly's, Lords of Uí Maine. It has interesting associations: with Boetius MacEgan, a Franciscan and bishop of the diocese of Elphin in the seventeenth century; and with St Ruth, the French commander, who was beheaded by a canonball at Aughrim's great disaster at the end of the Williamite wars. Or rather with his corpse, since it was said that the unfortunate man's remains were buried in Kilconnell. Another school of thought favours Loughrea, a few miles south-west of here.

In 1596 the friary was occupied for nine months by an English garrison which damaged neither friars nor friary. It is good to meditate on such happy, and exceptional, moments in history.

▽ Thoor Ballylee, Galway

The poet William Yeats, with 'old mill-boards and seagreen slates' and 'with smithy-work from the Gort forge, restored this tower' for his wife, George. The problems of housekeeping in such a place might not have been matter for poetry. But the tower, its history and its winding stair became symbols that the poet used with splendour when he was at the height of his soaring powers.

> I declare this tower is my symbol; I declare
> This winding, gyring, spiring treadmill of a stair
>   is my ancestral stair;
> That Goldsmith and the Dean, Berkeley and
>   Burke have travelled there.

He had also written, to end the inscription he wrote for the tower:

> And may these characters remain
> When all is ruin once again.

Ruin has been staved off by Michael Scott, the architect who also saved the Joyce tower which is now a museum, and by the late Molly O'Brien of Gort and her husband; and the symbol is now preserved by Bórd Fáilte, the Irish Tourist Board.

You are close to the lake and the seven woods of Coole where Lady Gregory's house was but, alas, is no longer.

Tawin Island, Galway ▷

Perhaps the most wonderful thing about Tawin Island in Galway Bay is that it is there at all. Seen from above it might easily appear that the sea is jealous of its existence. Seen on anything but a very large map, it is a speck, shaped somewhat like a tiny trowel yet still able to lord it over the smaller Eddy Island. Galway Bay is a very open space of water and not much given to islands, out of respect, perhaps, for the notable Aran Islands which more or less guard its mouth, but in and around Tawin is good ground and water for those self-effacing delicacies, the Galway oysters. Clarinbridge where, thirty or so years ago, the first Galway oyster festival opened, is in there on the shore, and beyond that there is Oranmore, renowned in the lovely song about the Galway shawl:

> She wore no jewels nor costly diamonds,
> Nor paint, nor powder, nor none at all.
> She wore a bonnet with red ribbons on it,
> And round her shoulders hung a Galway shawl.

In winter the island is famous for Brent geese.

In the early days of the Gaelic League it had a summer college, as such places were grandly called, where a young lady called Sinéad, and others, taught the native language. She married one of her most earnest students, a man by the name of Eamon de Valera.

There was once on the island a notice that said, 'Taking of stones prohibited'. One may readily see why. They think likewise in the low Lowlands of Holland.

Drumsna, Leitrim ▷

This is the Shannon riverine country at its most beautiful. Even down there on the ground you may appreciate on a calm evening how gently the light falls on the waters. In the distance are Bofin and Boderg, two of the lesser Shannon lakes, or expansions of the river. In the foreground is the village of Drumsna in which, or near which, one notable event happened: a great novelist found his vocation there or, at any rate, stepped on the springboard that set him off on his first novel. It were best to let him speak for himself:

I was located at a little town called Drumsna, or rather village, in the County Leitrim, where the postmaster had come to some sorrow about his money; and my friend John Merivale was staying with me for a day or two. As we were taking a walk in that most uninteresting country, we turned up through a deserted gateway, along a weedy, grass-grown avenue, till we came to the modern ruins of a country house. It was one of the most melancholy spots I ever visited. I will not describe it here, because I have done so in the first chapter of my first novel. We wandered about the place, and while I was still among the ruined walls and decayed beams I fabricated the plot of *The Macdermots of Ballycloren*. As to the plot itself, I do not know that I ever made one so good – or, at any rate, one so susceptible of pathos . . .

When my friend left me, I set to work and wrote the first chapter or two.

Good man, Mr Trollope of the Post Office.
Only to think that it all began in Drumsna.

Lough Allen, Leitrim ▷

Ireland's greatest river comes from a mystic pool, Shannon Pot, in the Cuilcagh mountains by Glangevlin, in the County Cavan, where all the McGoverns come from. It descends to meet a tributary bigger than itself, as can be the way with rivers, close to the village of Dowra. Then between Dowra and Drumshanbo, County Leitrim, it spreads out in the first of the great, many-islanded Shannon lakes, Loch Allen. Drumshanbo is one of the pleasantest small towns in Ireland.

▽ **Westport,** Mayo

Out there on the tip of Clew Bay, Westport is probably one of the best planned towns in Ireland. The credit is due to the family of the Marquess of Sligo and to James Wyatt whom they employed, round about 1780, and who graced the place with a tree-lined river walk where one could meditate forever, lulled by the sound of flowing water.

The great house, to be glimpsed to the right on a corner of the bay, has many treasures and is open to the public. In the background is the cone of the holy mountain, Croagh Patrick.

In the grounds of Westport House George Moore imagined the beginning of his 'joyous' book *A Storyteller's Holiday*.

The Corrib Canal, Mayo ▷

A footnote in Hardimans's *History of Galway* (1820), recently reprinted by Kenny of Galway, tells us:

> To open a communication between Killala and Galway by means of the Moy, Loughmask and Loughcorrib, was one of the practicable projects of those who were employed to survey the navigable rivers of Ireland in the early part of the eighteenth century, and, if carried into effect, would have proved a most important addition to the internal navigation of this country.

Not so long after that was written, and in the golden age of canals, and as a project for famine relief, the great work was manfully attempted. We have heard what happens to the best-laid plans and this one, alas, was laid on porous limestone. There are underground rivers between Lough Mask, (which we see) and Corrib.

The canal was cut, the water poured in and went down with a gurgle. But going north from Cong, the bank of the vanished waterway provides a beautiful walking place: and you may admire, even if with some melancholy, the lovely stonework around the locks.

Clew Bay from Croagh Patrick, Mayo

St Patrick, it is said, enjoyed this prospect during forty days of prayer and fasting. Or perhaps his mind and eyes were fixed on the heavens above him. But every year on Garland Sunday, or Lá Lughnasa, the day of the games of Lugh, the god of light, fervent pilgrims ascend the holy mountain to invoke the patronage of the saint. The best consideration of the mountain, the pilgrimage and the pre-Christian associations, is to be found in Máire MacNéill's vast work *The Festival of Lughnasa*, in which the learned author follows the survivals of the ancient Celtic festival of the first fruits of harvest from site to site all over Ireland.

For the ardent pilgrim, or for the merc climber, it is an experience of high wonder to ascend the 2,510 feet, rough going as you near the top, in darkness and mist, and to come to the moment of revelation when the clouds part and Clew Bay and all the islands are visible – all the way to Clare Island or, maybe to ultima Thule.

◁ **Ashford Castle,** Mayo

The great nineteenth-century baronial-style hotel of Ashford Castle (it was formerly a Guinness house) stands, as may be seen, in splendid countryside on the narrow strip of land that divides the north of Lough Corrib from Lough Mask. The advantages for fishermen, fine or coarse, need not be commented on. Spelunkers may also be happy: there are underground streams and limestone caves in the area. Antiquarians and archaeologists are drawn to the village of Cong and its monastic remains: the most precious relic, the Cross of Cong, is in the National Museum in Dublin.

There is no better centre for exploring the Joyce country to the west, and beyond to Connemara and Killary harbour and the mountains of Mayo.

Achill Sound, Mayo ▷

Never was there a lovelier day or wilder scenery; after we had cleared the river and opened the bay, a view of surpassing grandeur was presented. We were surrounded on every side by an amphitheatre of bold and endless hills, except where the opening to the Atlantic showed us the dark waters of a boundless ocean . . . and the light breeze rippled the long and measured undulations from the sea, and bore us gently towards Achill Island.

The bay was filled with mackerel and, consequently, it was crowded with seafowl. In clamorous groups the gulls were darting on the fish below, and an endless variety of puffins and cormorants were incessant in pursuit of the smaller fry which had attracted the shoals of mackerels from the deep.

But the wind was too scant, and the hooker's sailing not sufficiently fast, to allow us to take fish in any quantity. We occasionally, however caught a mackerel, and shot, among a number of waterfowl, a beautiful specimen of the sea hawk, which I shall endeavour to preserve . . .

The fish and the fowl were then in vast abundance. Nowadays some of us might think that it would have been better to preserve the sea hawk alive: but all that was 160 years ago and W.H.Maxwell, the novelist and founder of a type of Irish fiction, was on his way out from Blacksod to Achill Island, the ultimate corner of the wide county of Mayo. He was to write about it afterwards in his classical *Wild Sports of the West*. Nowadays, too, he could have crossed the fine bridge at Achill Sound to an island that has great scenic beauty and a mixed history.

146

▽ Boyle, Roscommon

The Boyle River comes down like a torrent, as its Gaelic name suggests, from Loch Gara, then settles peacefully and handsomely below the town of Boyle and enters the many islanded Loch Key (Cé), whose historical and literary associations are rich. In the centre of the picture are the ruins of Boyle Abbey, Mainistear na Buaille, a Cistercian foundation dating back to 1148. They are among the most impressive monastic remains in the country, and the MacDermots of Moylurg were its most important patrons – with the O Conors and O Haras.

Just a few miles away, on Castle Island in Loch Key, once the residence of the MacDermot, the *Annals of Loch Cé* – now in the library of Trinity College, Dublin – were copied by scribes in the sixteenth century from the book of the Duignans. W.B.Yeats had envisioned a dwelling-place on the island for mystics and poets, but it never did take shape.

The grounds of the Rockingham estate on the lakeshore and around the burned-out shell of Rockingham House contain a splendid public park.

◁ Bellacorick, Mayo

There's a lonely road through bogland to the lake at Carrowmore, wrote A.E. (George Russell), poet, philosopher, organizer of co-operative creameries, and one of the key figures in our literature in the early years of this century. In his capacity as organizer he had travelled those lonely Mayo roads as, indeed, he had travelled all the roads of Ireland and had also brooded mystically in quiet places where, he wrote, a sleeper there lies dreaming where the water laps the shore.

Round about the same period the playwright John Millington Synge and the painter Jack Butler Yeats, travelled in those parts then oddly known as the Congested Districts: which meant scarcity of land and too many people for the land to feed. There's a lot of land, not then blossoming like the rose, between Crossmolina and Belmullet on the coast, the last stop before Brooklyn.

Synge wrote about it and Jack Yeats drew something of what he saw. Synge wrote:

There is a curious change in the appearance of the country when one moves inland from the coast districts of Mayo to the congested portions of the inner edge of the country. In this place there are no longer the Erris tracts of bog or the tracts of stone of Connemara, but one sees everywhere low hills and small farms of poor land that is half turf-bog, already much cut away, and half narrow plots of grass or tillage ...

Not quite accurate even then, and Bellacorick (that smoke halfway to the mountains) and the like of it, drawing power from the bogs, were to bring new life to the lonely roads.

▽ **Sligo Town,** Sligo

From the part of the world I was reared in, the approach to Sligo town was one of continuous wonder: by train, in those days, along the islanded Lough Erne, into sight, finally, of Dartry Mountain, a genuine table mountain, standing up above Bundoran and the rolling Atlantic breakers. Then by road along the coast for twenty-two miles, cornering under bare Benbulben's head to the sight of the old harbour and the bridge over the Gar-avogue (the one in the bottom right-hand corner), and to the hospitality of Gray's Inn as it was fifty-six years ago.

It is one of the best-sited towns in Ireland. At times it seems to be a grey, brooding place but then more than seven hundred years of history are distilled into these old, ghost-crowded streets. The town has the ruins of an old priory (Dominican, 1253) known, as is the custom in such cases, as the Abbey. And the associated names are notable: O'Conor, de Burgo, O'Donnell, Fitzgerald, Bingham, Hamilton, Coote, Kingston, Sarsfield.

It is also a bright and business-like town and for long has had the reputation of being one of the best shopping towns in the west and north-west. It has also, every year, the Yeats Summer School. So that students, professors, poets and others, from all over the world, wander those streets and cross those bridges, and learn to love them.

◁ **Sligo Town and Lough Gill,** Sligo

The salmon may not be in the tides as they were of old, nor the creel creak in the cart that carried the take to Sligo town to be sold. But the Garavogue River still rushes down from Lough Gill to the sea, and Jack B. Yeats once said to a friend of mine that he learned to paint by leaning over the bridge in the heart of the town, and watching the Garavogue water burst over the weir.

You can hire a boat and row up the lake, your back turned to the way you are going so that the whole wonder of Lough Gill bursts on you all of a sudden. And the poetic associations are so strong and so many that you keep asking yourself: which came first, these places or the poet?

Lissadell, Carney, Sligo

The light of evening, Lissadell,
Great windows, open to the south,
Two girls in silk kimonos, both
Beautiful, one a gazelle.

The poet Yeats remembers how, as a young man, he visited the great house in the woods on the shore of Sligo Bay and talked with Constance and Eva, two daughters of the great house of Gore-Booth.

Eva became a poet of some distinction, and her sister, who married Count Casimir Markiewicz, was a painter, like her husband. (The pilasters around the walls of the dining room were painted, by Casimir, with a remarkable series of full-length portraits – of the family, the gamekeeper, the forester and the butler.) Constance was also a fighter for Irish freedom, a member of the first Dáil, and a friend of the Dublin poor.

It was the sisters' grandfather, Robert Gore-Booth, who built Lissadell, in 1830–5. In the billiard room is a banner presented to him in gratitude for his help to the poor during the Famine: he mortgaged his estate in order to be able to feed everyone for miles around.

Inishmurray, Sligo

On this island of Inishmurray, four miles out in Donegal Bay and off the Sligo coast, the ground is literally littered with the stones of the past, pagan stones and Christian stones, holy stones and cursing stones. But the island has suffered the common fate in our society of small islands and fringe areas, and the living people have gone.

The patron saint is Mo-Laisse or Laisren, and the Vikings looted, at the beginning of the ninth century, the place that he had founded. This island seems as old as any place in, or near Ireland, and the enigmatic silence of the past has settled down undisturbed.

The oddest stones on Inishmurray are the Clocha Breaca, or speckled stones, which are cursing stones. There is a story, enshrined by Lord Killanin and Professor Duigan in their copious *Shell Guide to Ireland*, that an English lady employed the stones to put a jinx on Adolf Hitler. Thought I, who knows, who knows? And the Tory islanders used the stones of Tory successfully against a British gunboat.

▽ **Benbulben,** Sligo

It dominates the landscape to the right of the road as you go from Sligo town to Bundoran and Donegal town. Because of its mythological and literary associations it takes precedence over its companions, Benweeskin, Truskmore and Dartry. It dominates particularly at Drumcliff, and just before the road crosses the river coming down from Glencar to the sea:

> Under Bare Ben Bulben's head
> In Drumcliff churchyard Yeats is laid.
> An ancestor was rector there
> Long years ago, a church stands near,
> By the road an ancient cross.
> No marble, no conventional phrase;

On limestone quarried near the spot
By his command these words are cut:

> *Cast a cold eye*
> *On life, on death.*
> *Horseman, pass by!*

In the Fiannuidheacht legends the pursuit of Gráinne, the golden, the beautiful, and of Diarmuid of the Lovespot, by the jealous Fionn MacCumhaill, ends on that mountain when Diarmuid is forever slain, Fionn allowing him to be killed by a wild boar, Diarmuid's taboo animal.

In the civil war of the 1920s there were deaths on that mountain. In a more recent year it has again looked down on tragedy.

Mullaghmore, Sligo ▷

On the horizon the mountains are, from left to right, Truskmore, Benweeskin and Benbulben. The road runs around them from Sligo town to Bundoran and Ballyshannon; and a few miles before it reaches Bundoran there's a byroad to the left leading to the great mound of Mullaghmore, the strand, the village, the little harbour. There were, in my time, horse races on the sands to the left, noted down, among other things, by the painter Jack B. Yeats.

It was a happy place, untouched, you might have said, by the world, until the brutal murder there of Earl Mountbatten on the waters to the left.

The black spot to the right is Classiebawn Castle where he sometimes lived.

'Once every few months I used to go to Rosses Point or Ballisodare to see another little boy who had a piebald pony that was once in a circus and sometimes forgot where it was and went round and round.'

That was William Butler Yeats in his *Reveries over Childhood and Youth*, writing about his little corner of the Sligo coast and about his relative, little George Middleton, who owned the absent-minded pony.

So, in honour of Yeats, we may walk the road out of Sligo town, and turn left into this quiet corner that guards the entrance into Sligo harbour. The passing that way of a great poet has given it another dignity.

Keshcorran, Sligo ▷

This impressive and somewhat sinister mountain, Keshcorran, the Hog of Corran, dominates the road from Boyle, County Roscommon, to Ballymote, County Sligo.

Corran, the harper, made such beautiful music for the enchanted people, the Tuatha de Danaan, that they gave him all the fertile plain that lies to the west of the mountain.

Diarmuid and Gráinne came here in their flight before the anger of Fionn, and Diarmuid, through his sleep, heard the cry of the hounds and went out to meet his death on Benbulben.

From that Boyle-Ballymote road the mountain has a somewhat monstrous appearance because of the gaping mouths of the caves of Kesh, in which bits of the bones of wild animals have been found.

In a long meadow at the foot of the mountain our forebears have met since God knows when to celebrate the midsummer games of Lugh, the god of light, and the dark god, Crom Dubh: and, in our own time, Garland Sunday on the last weekend in July continues the tradition.

Index